Market Insights Leaders
Complete Self-Assessment Guide

The guidance in this Self-Assessment is based on Market Insights Leaders best practices and standards in business process architecture, design and quality management. The guidance is also based on the professional judgment of the individual collaborators listed in the Acknowledgments.

Notice of rights

You are licensed to use the Self-Assessment contents in your presentations and materials for internal use and customers without asking us - we are here to help.

Trademarks

Table of Contents

About The Art of Service

The Art of Service, Business Process Architects since 2000, is dedicated to helping stakeholders achieve excellence.

Defining, designing, creating, and implementing a process to solve a stakeholders challenge or meet an objective is the most valuable role… In EVERY group, company, organization and department.

Unless you're talking a one-time, single-use project, there should be a process. Whether that process is managed and implemented by humans, AI, or a combination of the two, it needs to be designed by someone with a complex enough perspective to ask the right questions.

Someone capable of asking the right questions and step back and say, 'What are we really trying to accomplish here? And is there a different way to look at it?'

With The Art of Service's Standard Requirements Self-Assessments, we empower people who can do just that — whether their title is marketer, entrepreneur, manager, salesperson, consultant, Business Process Manager, executive assistant, IT Manager, CIO etc... —they are the people who rule the future. They are people who watch the process as it happens, and ask the right questions to make the process work better.

Contact us when you need any support with this Self-Assessment and any help with templates, blue-prints and examples of standard documents you might need:

http://theartofservice.com
service@theartofservice.com

Included Resources - how to access

Included with your purchase of the book is the Market Insights

Leaders Self-Assessment Spreadsheet Dashboard which contains all questions and Self-Assessment areas and auto-generates insights, graphs, and project RACI planning - all with examples to get you started right away.

How? Simply send an email to
access@theartofservice.com
with this books' title in the subject to get the Market Insights Leaders Self Assessment Tool right away.

You will receive the following contents with New and Updated specific criteria:

- The latest quick edition of the book in PDF

- The latest complete edition of the book in PDF, which criteria correspond to the criteria in...

- The Self-Assessment Excel Dashboard, and...

- Example pre-filled Self-Assessment Excel Dashboard to get familiar with results generation

- In-depth specific Checklists covering the topic

- Project management checklists and templates to assist with implementation

Purpose of this Self-Assessment

This Self-Assessment has been developed to improve understanding of the requirements and elements of Market Insights Leaders, based on best practices and standards in business process architecture, design and quality management.

It is designed to allow for a rapid Self-Assessment to determine how closely existing management practices and procedures correspond to the elements of the Self-Assessment.

The criteria of requirements and elements of Market Insights Leaders have been rephrased in the format of a Self-Assessment questionnaire, with a seven-criterion scoring system, as explained in this document.

In this format, even with limited background knowledge of Market Insights Leaders, a manager can quickly review existing operations to determine how they measure up to the standards. This in turn can serve as the starting point of a 'gap analysis' to identify management tools or system elements that might usefully be implemented in the organization to help improve overall performance.

How to use the Self-Assessment

On the following pages are a series of questions to identify to what extent your Market Insights Leaders initiative is complete in comparison to the requirements set in standards.

To facilitate answering the questions, there is a space in front of each question to enter a score on a scale of '1' to '5'.

1 Strongly Disagree

2 Disagree

3 Neutral

4 Agree

5 Strongly Agree

Read the question and rate it with the following in front of mind:

'In my belief,
the answer to this question is clearly defined'.

There are two ways in which you can choose to interpret this statement;
1. how aware are you that the answer to the question is clearly defined
2. for more in-depth analysis you can choose to gather evidence and confirm the answer to the question. This obviously will take more time, most Self-Assessment users opt for the first way to interpret the question and dig deeper later on based on the outcome of the overall Self-Assessment.

A score of '1' would mean that the answer is not clear at all, where a '5' would mean the answer is crystal clear and defined. Leave emtpy when the question is not applicable or you don't want to answer it, you can skip it without affecting your score. Write your score in the space provided.

After you have responded to all the appropriate statements in each section, compute your average score for that section, using the formula provided, and round to the nearest tenth. Then transfer to the corresponding spoke in the Market Insights Leaders Scorecard on the second next page of the Self-Assessment.

Your completed Market Insights Leaders Scorecard will give you a clear presentation of which Market Insights Leaders areas need attention.

Market Insights Leaders Scorecard Example

Example of how the finalized Scorecard can look like:

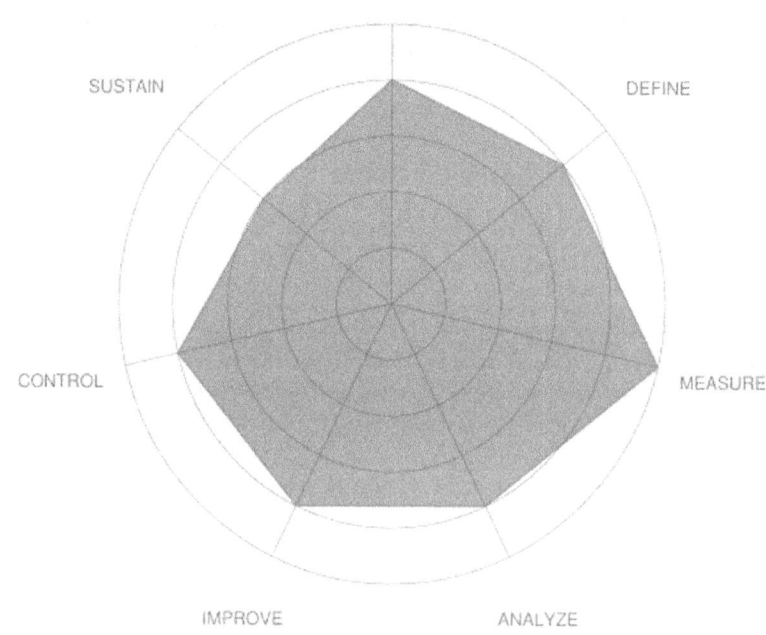

Market Insights Leaders Scorecard

Your Scores:

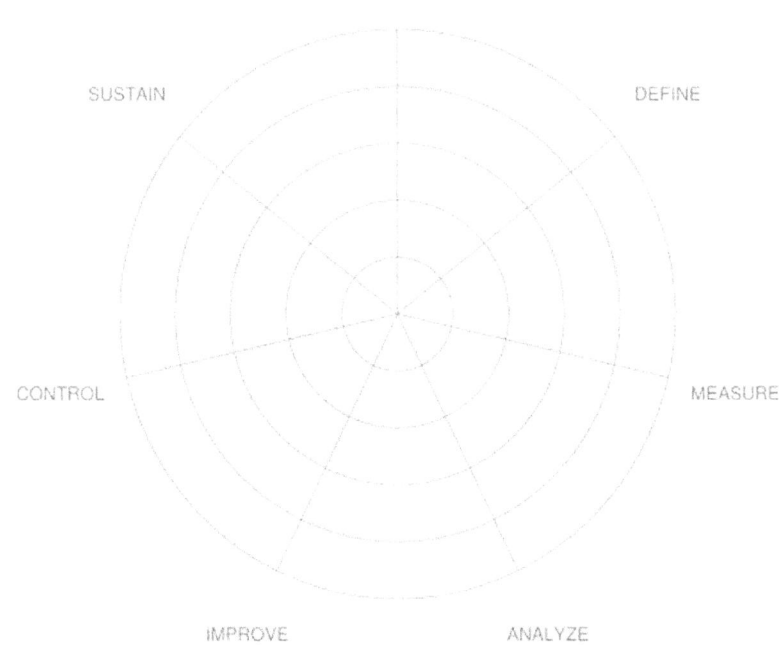

BEGINNING OF THE SELF-ASSESSMENT:

CRITERION #1: RECOGNIZE

INTENT: Be aware of the need for change. Recognize that there is an unfavorable variation, problem or symptom.

In my belief, the answer to this question is clearly defined:

5 Strongly Agree

4 Agree

3 Neutral

2 Disagree

1 Strongly Disagree

1. How can auditing be a preventative security measure?
<--- Score

2. Are there any specific expectations or concerns about the Market insights leaders team, Market insights leaders itself?
<--- Score

3. What needs to be done?
<--- Score

4. To what extent would your organization benefit from being recognized as a award recipient?
<--- Score

5. What are the stakeholder objectives to be achieved with Market insights leaders?
<--- Score

6. What is the extent or complexity of the Market insights leaders problem?
<--- Score

7. What do employees need in the short term?
<--- Score

8. Is the need for organizational change recognized?
<--- Score

9. Who defines the rules in relation to any given issue?
<--- Score

10. What else needs to be measured?
<--- Score

11. Will Market insights leaders deliverables need to be tested and, if so, by whom?
<--- Score

12. Do you have/need 24-hour access to key personnel?
<--- Score

13. Are employees recognized for desired behaviors?

<--- Score

14. Where do you need to exercise leadership?

<--- Score

15. What is the problem and/or vulnerability?

<--- Score

16. What Market insights leaders events should you attend?

<--- Score

17. Does your organization need more Market insights leaders education?

<--- Score

18. Who needs to know?

<--- Score

19. Think about the people you identified for your Market insights leaders project and the project responsibilities you would assign to them, what kind of training do you think they would need to perform these responsibilities effectively?

<--- Score

20. Are controls defined to recognize and contain problems?

<--- Score

21. Why the need?

<--- Score

22. What are the minority interests and what amount of minority interests can be recognized?
<--- Score

23. Which issues are too important to ignore?
<--- Score

24. Would you recognize a threat from the inside?
<--- Score

25. How does it fit into your organizational needs and tasks?
<--- Score

26. What is the problem or issue?
<--- Score

27. What is the recognized need?
<--- Score

28. Do you need to avoid or amend any Market insights leaders activities?
<--- Score

29. What are the clients issues and concerns?
<--- Score

30. Which information does the Market insights leaders business case need to include?
<--- Score

31. Will a response program recognize when a crisis occurs and provide some level of response?
<--- Score

32. Are employees recognized or rewarded for

performance that demonstrates the highest levels of integrity?
<--- Score

33. How do you recognize an objection?
<--- Score

34. Are you dealing with any of the same issues today as yesterday? What can you do about this?
<--- Score

35. What situation(s) led to this Market insights leaders Self Assessment?
<--- Score

36. What activities does the governance board need to consider?
<--- Score

37. How much are sponsors, customers, partners, stakeholders involved in Market insights leaders? In other words, what are the risks, if Market insights leaders does not deliver successfully?
<--- Score

38. What are the Market insights leaders resources needed?
<--- Score

39. Do you know what you need to know about Market insights leaders?
<--- Score

40. How are you going to measure success?
<--- Score

41. What resources or support might you need?
<--- Score

42. When a Market insights leaders manager recognizes a problem, what options are available?
<--- Score

43. What prevents you from making the changes you know will make you a more effective Market insights leaders leader?
<--- Score

44. How do you assess your Market insights leaders workforce capability and capacity needs, including skills, competencies, and staffing levels?
<--- Score

45. What Market insights leaders capabilities do you need?
<--- Score

46. How do you recognize an Market insights leaders objection?
<--- Score

47. Are your goals realistic? Do you need to redefine your problem? Perhaps the problem has changed or maybe you have reached your goal and need to set a new one?
<--- Score

48. What do you need to start doing?
<--- Score

49. Are there any revenue recognition issues?
<--- Score

50. What creative shifts do you need to take?
<--- Score

51. Where is training needed?
<--- Score

52. Who needs to know about Market insights leaders?
<--- Score

53. Are there Market insights leaders problems defined?
<--- Score

54. Will it solve real problems?
<--- Score

55. What training and capacity building actions are needed to implement proposed reforms?
<--- Score

56. What Market insights leaders problem should be solved?
<--- Score

57. Who should resolve the Market insights leaders issues?
<--- Score

58. What is the smallest subset of the problem you can usefully solve?
<--- Score

59. Have you identified your Market insights leaders key performance indicators?

<--- Score

60. How do you identify subcontractor relationships?
<--- Score

61. Are problem definition and motivation clearly presented?
<--- Score

62. How are the Market insights leaders's objectives aligned to the group's overall stakeholder strategy?
<--- Score

63. Are there regulatory / compliance issues?
<--- Score

64. Is it clear when you think of the day ahead of you what activities and tasks you need to complete?
<--- Score

65. What extra resources will you need?
<--- Score

66. Is it needed?
<--- Score

67. How many trainings, in total, are needed?
<--- Score

68. What problems are you facing and how do you consider Market insights leaders will circumvent those obstacles?
<--- Score

69. What tools and technologies are needed for a

custom Market insights leaders project?
<--- Score

70. Does the problem have ethical dimensions?
<--- Score

71. Does Market insights leaders create potential expectations in other areas that need to be recognized and considered?
<--- Score

72. What needs to stay?
<--- Score

73. Whom do you really need or want to serve?
<--- Score

74. Are losses recognized in a timely manner?
<--- Score

75. Who are your key stakeholders who need to sign off?
<--- Score

76. For your Market insights leaders project, identify and describe the business environment, is there more than one layer to the business environment?
<--- Score

77. Who needs budgets?
<--- Score

78. What would happen if Market insights leaders weren't done?
<--- Score

79. Will new equipment/products be required to facilitate Market insights leaders delivery, for example is new software needed?
<--- Score

80. How do you identify the kinds of information that you will need?
<--- Score

81. What does Market insights leaders success mean to the stakeholders?
<--- Score

82. Who needs what information?
<--- Score

83. What are the timeframes required to resolve each of the issues/problems?
<--- Score

84. What vendors make products that address the Market insights leaders needs?
<--- Score

85. As a sponsor, customer or management, how important is it to meet goals, objectives?
<--- Score

86. How do you take a forward-looking perspective in identifying Market insights leaders research related to market response and models?
<--- Score

87. What information do users need?
<--- Score

88. What are the expected benefits of Market insights leaders to the stakeholder?
<--- Score

89. Why is this needed?
<--- Score

90. Consider your own Market insights leaders project, what types of organizational problems do you think might be causing or affecting your problem, based on the work done so far?
<--- Score

91. What Market insights leaders coordination do you need?
<--- Score

92. What should be considered when identifying available resources, constraints, and deadlines?
<--- Score

93. Which needs are not included or involved?
<--- Score

94. Who else hopes to benefit from it?
<--- Score

95. To what extent does each concerned units management team recognize Market insights leaders as an effective investment?
<--- Score

Add up total points for this section:
_ _ _ _ _ = Total points for this section

Divided by: _ _ _ _ _ _ (number of

statements answered) = _ _ _ _ _ _
Average score for this section

Transfer your score to the Market
insights leaders Index at the beginning
of the Self-Assessment.

CRITERION #2: DEFINE:

INTENT: Formulate the stakeholder problem. Define the problem, needs and objectives.

In my belief, the answer to this question is clearly defined:

5 Strongly Agree

4 Agree

3 Neutral

2 Disagree

1 Strongly Disagree

1. How will the Market insights leaders team and the group measure complete success of Market insights leaders?
<--- Score

2. What critical content must be communicated – who, what, when, where, and how?
<--- Score

3. Has everyone on the team, including the team leaders, been properly trained?
<--- Score

4. What are the core elements of the Market insights leaders business case?
<--- Score

5. In what way can you redefine the criteria of choice clients have in your category in your favor?
<--- Score

6. When are meeting minutes sent out? Who is on the distribution list?
<--- Score

7. What are the Market insights leaders use cases?
<--- Score

8. Does the team have regular meetings?
<--- Score

9. Is the Market insights leaders scope manageable?
<--- Score

10. How would you define Market insights leaders leadership?
<--- Score

11. Has a project plan, Gantt chart, or similar been developed/completed?
<--- Score

12. Has the improvement team collected the 'voice of the customer' (obtained feedback – qualitative and quantitative)?

<--- Score

13. Is there a critical path to deliver Market insights leaders results?
<--- Score

14. What are the rough order estimates on cost savings/opportunities that Market insights leaders brings?
<--- Score

15. Is there a Market insights leaders management charter, including stakeholder case, problem and goal statements, scope, milestones, roles and responsibilities, communication plan?
<--- Score

16. Why are you doing Market insights leaders and what is the scope?
<--- Score

17. What are the Market insights leaders tasks and definitions?
<--- Score

18. What sources do you use to gather information for a Market insights leaders study?
<--- Score

19. Is Market insights leaders linked to key stakeholder goals and objectives?
<--- Score

20. What are (control) requirements for Market insights leaders Information?
<--- Score

21. How do you gather requirements?
<--- Score

22. How does the Market insights leaders manager ensure against scope creep?
<--- Score

23. Are approval levels defined for contracts and supplements to contracts?
<--- Score

24. How are consistent Market insights leaders definitions important?
<--- Score

25. How will variation in the actual durations of each activity be dealt with to ensure that the expected Market insights leaders results are met?
<--- Score

26. What is the scope of Market insights leaders?
<--- Score

27. How and when will the baselines be defined?
<--- Score

28. What specifically is the problem? Where does it occur? When does it occur? What is its extent?
<--- Score

29. What constraints exist that might impact the team?
<--- Score

30. How do you think the partners involved in Market

insights leaders would have defined success?
<--- Score

31. Has a Market insights leaders requirement not been met?
<--- Score

32. How was the 'as is' process map developed, reviewed, verified and validated?
<--- Score

33. Are the Market insights leaders requirements complete?
<--- Score

34. Is the scope of Market insights leaders defined?
<--- Score

35. How do you keep key subject matter experts in the loop?
<--- Score

36. How often are the team meetings?
<--- Score

37. Has your scope been defined?
<--- Score

38. Does the scope remain the same?
<--- Score

39. What are the tasks and definitions?
<--- Score

40. How do you manage unclear Market insights leaders requirements?

<--- Score

41. The political context: who holds power?
<--- Score

42. What was the context?
<--- Score

43. What customer feedback methods were used to solicit their input?
<--- Score

44. How have you defined all Market insights leaders requirements first?
<--- Score

45. Is there a completed SIPOC representation, describing the Suppliers, Inputs, Process, Outputs, and Customers?
<--- Score

46. How do you manage changes in Market insights leaders requirements?
<--- Score

47. What would be the goal or target for a Market insights leaders's improvement team?
<--- Score

48. Are different versions of process maps needed to account for the different types of inputs?
<--- Score

49. What are the Roles and Responsibilities for each team member and its leadership? Where is this documented?

<--- Score

50. Has a high-level 'as is' process map been completed, verified and validated?
<--- Score

51. Do the problem and goal statements meet the SMART criteria (specific, measurable, attainable, relevant, and time-bound)?
<--- Score

52. What sort of initial information to gather?
<--- Score

53. Is the current 'as is' process being followed? If not, what are the discrepancies?
<--- Score

54. Has the direction changed at all during the course of Market insights leaders? If so, when did it change and why?
<--- Score

55. Is data collected and displayed to better understand customer(s) critical needs and requirements.
<--- Score

56. How do you build the right business case?
<--- Score

57. Are accountability and ownership for Market insights leaders clearly defined?
<--- Score

58. Who approved the Market insights leaders

scope?
<--- Score

59. Is special Market insights leaders user knowledge required?
<--- Score

60. Who are the Market insights leaders improvement team members, including Management Leads and Coaches?
<--- Score

61. What is a worst-case scenario for losses?
<--- Score

62. Are roles and responsibilities formally defined?
<--- Score

63. How would you define the culture at your organization, how susceptible is it to Market insights leaders changes?
<--- Score

64. Is there regularly 100% attendance at the team meetings? If not, have appointed substitutes attended to preserve cross-functionality and full representation?
<--- Score

65. Do you have a Market insights leaders success story or case study ready to tell and share?
<--- Score

66. What is out of scope?
<--- Score

67. How do you catch Market insights leaders definition inconsistencies?
<--- Score

68. Do you have organizational privacy requirements?
<--- Score

69. How is the team tracking and documenting its work?
<--- Score

70. How do you hand over Market insights leaders context?
<--- Score

71. Is there a clear Market insights leaders case definition?
<--- Score

72. Who defines (or who defined) the rules and roles?
<--- Score

73. What baselines are required to be defined and managed?
<--- Score

74. Is Market insights leaders required?
<--- Score

75. Who is gathering Market insights leaders information?
<--- Score

76. What scope do you want your strategy to cover?
<--- Score

77. Has/have the customer(s) been identified?
<--- Score

78. What Market insights leaders requirements should be gathered?
<--- Score

79. When is the estimated completion date?
<--- Score

80. How do you gather Market insights leaders requirements?
<--- Score

81. Are customer(s) identified and segmented according to their different needs and requirements?
<--- Score

82. What key stakeholder process output measure(s) does Market insights leaders leverage and how?
<--- Score

83. What defines best in class?
<--- Score

84. What is out-of-scope initially?
<--- Score

85. Do you all define Market insights leaders in the same way?
<--- Score

86. Is the improvement team aware of the different versions of a process: what they think it is vs. what it actually is vs. what it should be vs. what it could be?
<--- Score

87. What is the definition of success?
<--- Score

88. What are the requirements for audit information?
<--- Score

89. What information should you gather?
<--- Score

90. What are the dynamics of the communication plan?
<--- Score

91. Is the work to date meeting requirements?
<--- Score

92. Has anyone else (internal or external to the group) attempted to solve this problem or a similar one before? If so, what knowledge can be leveraged from these previous efforts?
<--- Score

93. Has a team charter been developed and communicated?
<--- Score

94. What information do you gather?
<--- Score

95. Has the Market insights leaders work been fairly and/or equitably divided and delegated among team members who are qualified and capable to perform the work? Has everyone contributed?
<--- Score

96. Have specific policy objectives been defined?
<--- Score

97. What intelligence can you gather?
<--- Score

98. What are the record-keeping requirements of Market insights leaders activities?
<--- Score

99. Is the team adequately staffed with the desired cross-functionality? If not, what additional resources are available to the team?
<--- Score

100. Are all requirements met?
<--- Score

101. Scope of sensitive information?
<--- Score

102. Are task requirements clearly defined?
<--- Score

103. When is/was the Market insights leaders start date?
<--- Score

104. Are there different segments of customers?
<--- Score

105. What is the scope of the Market insights leaders work?
<--- Score

106. Have the customer needs been translated into

specific, measurable requirements? How?
<--- Score

107. Is scope creep really all bad news?
<--- Score

108. What is in scope?
<--- Score

109. Who is gathering information?
<--- Score

110. What knowledge or experience is required?
<--- Score

111. Is it clearly defined in and to your organization what you do?
<--- Score

112. How do you manage scope?
<--- Score

113. Is there any additional Market insights leaders definition of success?
<--- Score

114. Where can you gather more information?
<--- Score

115. What system do you use for gathering Market insights leaders information?
<--- Score

116. Are resources adequate for the scope?
<--- Score

117. Is Market insights leaders currently on schedule according to the plan?
<--- Score

118. Is there a completed, verified, and validated high-level 'as is' (not 'should be' or 'could be') stakeholder process map?
<--- Score

119. Are there any constraints known that bear on the ability to perform Market insights leaders work? How is the team addressing them?
<--- Score

120. What is the scope of the Market insights leaders effort?
<--- Score

121. Are required metrics defined, what are they?
<--- Score

122. What gets examined?
<--- Score

123. If substitutes have been appointed, have they been briefed on the Market insights leaders goals and received regular communications as to the progress to date?
<--- Score

124. What are the boundaries of the scope? What is in bounds and what is not? What is the start point? What is the stop point?
<--- Score

125. What is the context?

<--- Score

126. How can the value of Market insights leaders be defined?
<--- Score

127. What scope to assess?
<--- Score

128. What are the compelling stakeholder reasons for embarking on Market insights leaders?
<--- Score

129. Are the Market insights leaders requirements testable?
<--- Score

130. Have all basic functions of Market insights leaders been defined?
<--- Score

131. How did the Market insights leaders manager receive input to the development of a Market insights leaders improvement plan and the estimated completion dates/times of each activity?
<--- Score

132. What is the worst case scenario?
<--- Score

133. What is the definition of Market insights leaders excellence?
<--- Score

Add up total points for this section:
_ _ _ _ _ = Total points for this section

Divided by: _____ (number of
statements answered) = _____
Average score for this section

Transfer your score to the Market
insights leaders Index at the beginning
of the Self-Assessment.

CRITERION #3: MEASURE:

INTENT: Gather the correct data.
Measure the current performance and
evolution of the situation.

In my belief, the answer to this
question is clearly defined:

5 Strongly Agree

4 Agree

3 Neutral

2 Disagree

1 Strongly Disagree

1. How much does it cost?
<--- Score

2. What harm might be caused?
<--- Score

3. What are the Market insights leaders investment costs?
<--- Score

4. How do you control the overall costs of your work processes?
<--- Score

5. Have you made assumptions about the shape of the future, particularly its impact on your customers and competitors?
<--- Score

6. What would be a real cause for concern?
<--- Score

7. How do you quantify and qualify impacts?
<--- Score

8. How will you measure success?
<--- Score

9. What users will be impacted?
<--- Score

10. Does the Market insights leaders task fit the client's priorities?
<--- Score

11. How is performance measured?
<--- Score

12. Are there competing Market insights leaders priorities?
<--- Score

13. How can you reduce costs?
<--- Score

14. Is it possible to estimate the impact of unanticipated complexity such as wrong or failed assumptions, feedback, etcetera on proposed reforms?
<--- Score

15. What are the current costs of the Market insights leaders process?
<--- Score

16. How do you measure efficient delivery of Market insights leaders services?
<--- Score

17. When are costs are incurred?
<--- Score

18. What evidence is there and what is measured?
<--- Score

19. Was a business case (cost/benefit) developed?
<--- Score

20. How do you measure lifecycle phases?
<--- Score

21. Are there any easy-to-implement alternatives to Market insights leaders? Sometimes other solutions are available that do not require the cost implications of a full-blown project?
<--- Score

22. What is the Market insights leaders business impact?
<--- Score

23. What could cause you to change course?
<--- Score

24. Did you tackle the cause or the symptom?
<--- Score

25. How can you measure Market insights leaders in a systematic way?
<--- Score

26. What are your operating costs?
<--- Score

27. What is the root cause(s) of the problem?
<--- Score

28. When a disaster occurs, who gets priority?
<--- Score

29. How is progress measured?
<--- Score

30. How do your measurements capture actionable Market insights leaders information for use in exceeding your customers expectations and securing your customers engagement?
<--- Score

31. How will costs be allocated?
<--- Score

32. How will your organization measure success?
<--- Score

33. Are supply costs steady or fluctuating?
<--- Score

34. What are the estimated costs of proposed changes?
<--- Score

35. What do people want to verify?
<--- Score

36. What happens if cost savings do not materialize?
<--- Score

37. What methods are feasible and acceptable to estimate the impact of reforms?
<--- Score

38. How can a Market insights leaders test verify your ideas or assumptions?
<--- Score

39. How frequently do you track Market insights leaders measures?
<--- Score

40. What would it cost to replace your technology?
<--- Score

41. Are indirect costs charged to the Market insights leaders program?
<--- Score

42. Among the Market insights leaders product and service cost to be estimated, which is considered hardest to estimate?
<--- Score

43. Are Market insights leaders vulnerabilities

categorized and prioritized?
<--- Score

44. How do you verify if Market insights leaders is built right?
<--- Score

45. How do you verify your resources?
<--- Score

46. How long to keep data and how to manage retention costs?
<--- Score

47. How can you reduce the costs of obtaining inputs?
<--- Score

48. What are allowable costs?
<--- Score

49. Do you have any cost Market insights leaders limitation requirements?
<--- Score

50. Which measures and indicators matter?
<--- Score

51. Are you aware of what could cause a problem?
<--- Score

52. What can be used to verify compliance?
<--- Score

53. What are hidden Market insights leaders quality costs?

<--- Score

54. What could cause delays in the schedule?
<--- Score

55. When should you bother with diagrams?
<--- Score

56. Who pays the cost?
<--- Score

57. What are the costs of delaying Market insights leaders action?
<--- Score

58. Has a cost center been established?
<--- Score

59. Does management have the right priorities among projects?
<--- Score

60. How do you aggregate measures across priorities?
<--- Score

61. How will effects be measured?
<--- Score

62. What are the uncertainties surrounding estimates of impact?
<--- Score

63. What disadvantage does this cause for the user?
<--- Score

64. Is the cost worth the Market insights leaders effort ?
<--- Score

65. How will success or failure be measured?
<--- Score

66. What causes innovation to fail or succeed in your organization?
<--- Score

67. How do you verify the authenticity of the data and information used?
<--- Score

68. Are there measurements based on task performance?
<--- Score

69. What are your customers expectations and measures?
<--- Score

70. What causes mismanagement?
<--- Score

71. What details are required of the Market insights leaders cost structure?
<--- Score

72. How do you verify the Market insights leaders requirements quality?
<--- Score

73. Do you effectively measure and reward individual and team performance?

<--- Score

74. How do you measure variability?
<--- Score

75. How do you verify performance?
<--- Score

76. How do you verify and develop ideas and innovations?
<--- Score

77. Do you aggressively reward and promote the people who have the biggest impact on creating excellent Market insights leaders services/products?
<--- Score

78. Have you included everything in your Market insights leaders cost models?
<--- Score

79. How can you manage cost down?
<--- Score

80. What relevant entities could be measured?
<--- Score

81. What are the costs and benefits?
<--- Score

82. Are the units of measure consistent?
<--- Score

83. What potential environmental factors impact the Market insights leaders effort?
<--- Score

84. How sensitive must the Market insights leaders strategy be to cost?
<--- Score

85. Do you have an issue in getting priority?
<--- Score

86. Are the Market insights leaders benefits worth its costs?
<--- Score

87. How are costs allocated?
<--- Score

88. Where is it measured?
<--- Score

89. Have design-to-cost goals been established?
<--- Score

90. How will you measure your Market insights leaders effectiveness?
<--- Score

91. What is measured? Why?
<--- Score

92. At what cost?
<--- Score

93. What causes extra work or rework?
<--- Score

94. Do you have a flow diagram of what happens?
<--- Score

95. What measurements are being captured?

<--- Score

96. Why do you expend time and effort to implement measurement, for whom?

<--- Score

97. What are the Market insights leaders key cost drivers?

<--- Score

98. How can you measure the performance?

<--- Score

99. What drives O&M cost?

<--- Score

100. What does losing customers cost your organization?

<--- Score

101. Does a Market insights leaders quantification method exist?

<--- Score

102. What tests verify requirements?

<--- Score

103. Which costs should be taken into account?

<--- Score

104. What is the cause of any Market insights leaders gaps?

<--- Score

105. How is the value delivered by Market insights leaders being measured?
<--- Score

106. What is your Market insights leaders quality cost segregation study?
<--- Score

107. Is the solution cost-effective?
<--- Score

108. How to cause the change?
<--- Score

109. What is an unallowable cost?
<--- Score

110. What are the costs?
<--- Score

111. Are you able to realize any cost savings?
<--- Score

112. How will measures be used to manage and adapt?
<--- Score

113. Is there an opportunity to verify requirements?
<--- Score

114. What causes investor action?
<--- Score

115. What are your key Market insights leaders organizational performance measures, including key short and longer-term financial measures?

<--- Score

116. Are the measurements objective?
<--- Score

117. What are you verifying?
<--- Score

118. What measurements are possible, practicable and meaningful?
<--- Score

119. What are the types and number of measures to use?
<--- Score

120. What are the costs of reform?
<--- Score

121. How do you prevent mis-estimating cost?
<--- Score

122. Why do the measurements/indicators matter?
<--- Score

123. What are the strategic priorities for this year?
<--- Score

124. What is your decision requirements diagram?
<--- Score

125. How are measurements made?
<--- Score

126. How do you measure success?
<--- Score

127. What does your operating model cost?
<--- Score

128. What are the operational costs after Market insights leaders deployment?
<--- Score

129. What are your primary costs, revenues, assets?
<--- Score

130. Are you taking your company in the direction of better and revenue or cheaper and cost?
<--- Score

131. What does a Test Case verify?
<--- Score

Add up total points for this section:
_ _ _ _ _ = Total points for this section

Divided by: _ _ _ _ _ _ (number of statements answered) = _ _ _ _ _ _
Average score for this section

Transfer your score to the Market insights leaders Index at the beginning of the Self-Assessment.

CRITERION #4: ANALYZE:

INTENT: Analyze causes, assumptions and hypotheses.

In my belief, the answer to this question is clearly defined:

5 Strongly Agree

4 Agree

3 Neutral

2 Disagree

1 Strongly Disagree

1. Do staff qualifications match your project?
<--- Score

2. How will corresponding data be collected?
<--- Score

3. What qualifies as competition?
<--- Score

4. What are evaluation criteria for the output?

<--- Score

5. How can risk management be tied procedurally to process elements?
<--- Score

6. Who will gather what data?
<--- Score

7. Where can you get qualified talent today?
<--- Score

8. What other jobs or tasks affect the performance of the steps in the Market insights leaders process?
<--- Score

9. Do your contracts/agreements contain data security obligations?
<--- Score

10. What successful thing are you doing today that may be blinding you to new growth opportunities?
<--- Score

11. Do your leaders quickly bounce back from setbacks?
<--- Score

12. Were Pareto charts (or similar) used to portray the 'heavy hitters' (or key sources of variation)?
<--- Score

13. How is data used for program management and improvement?
<--- Score

14. What are the personnel training and qualifications required?

<--- Score

15. What Market insights leaders data will be collected?

<--- Score

16. What are the Market insights leaders design outputs?

<--- Score

17. Where is the data coming from to measure compliance?

<--- Score

18. What controls do you have in place to protect data?

<--- Score

19. What training and qualifications will you need?

<--- Score

20. How does the organization define, manage, and improve its Market insights leaders processes?

<--- Score

21. What do you need to qualify?

<--- Score

22. What does the data say about the performance of the stakeholder process?

<--- Score

23. How do you promote understanding that opportunity for improvement is not criticism of

the status quo, or the people who created the status quo?
<--- Score

24. Who gets your output?
<--- Score

25. What is the Value Stream Mapping?
<--- Score

26. Was a cause-and-effect diagram used to explore the different types of causes (or sources of variation)?
<--- Score

27. Who qualifies to gain access to data?
<--- Score

28. Do you, as a leader, bounce back quickly from setbacks?
<--- Score

29. Should you invest in industry-recognized qualifications?
<--- Score

30. How do mission and objectives affect the Market insights leaders processes of your organization?
<--- Score

31. What tools were used to generate the list of possible causes?
<--- Score

32. How much data can be collected in the given timeframe?
<--- Score

33. How do you use Market insights leaders data and information to support organizational decision making and innovation?
<--- Score

34. What systems/processes must you excel at?
<--- Score

35. What were the financial benefits resulting from any 'ground fruit or low-hanging fruit' (quick fixes)?
<--- Score

36. What qualifications are necessary?
<--- Score

37. Think about some of the processes you undertake within your organization, which do you own?
<--- Score

38. What qualifications and skills do you need?
<--- Score

39. How many input/output points does it require?
<--- Score

40. What were the crucial 'moments of truth' on the process map?
<--- Score

41. What is your organizations system for selecting qualified vendors?
<--- Score

42. Do quality systems drive continuous improvement?

<--- Score

43. How difficult is it to qualify what Market insights leaders ROI is?
<--- Score

44. What are the necessary qualifications?
<--- Score

45. What quality tools were used to get through the analyze phase?
<--- Score

46. Are all team members qualified for all tasks?
<--- Score

47. What are the disruptive Market insights leaders technologies that enable your organization to radically change your business processes?
<--- Score

48. Are Market insights leaders changes recognized early enough to be approved through the regular process?
<--- Score

49. Has data output been validated?
<--- Score

50. What is the complexity of the output produced?
<--- Score

51. What are your Market insights leaders processes?
<--- Score

52. Are you missing Market insights leaders

opportunities?
<--- Score

53. What process should you select for improvement?
<--- Score

54. What tools were used to narrow the list of possible causes?
<--- Score

55. What Market insights leaders data should be collected?
<--- Score

56. Is there any way to speed up the process?
<--- Score

57. What internal processes need improvement?
<--- Score

58. How do you define collaboration and team output?
<--- Score

59. What resources go in to get the desired output?
<--- Score

60. What is the oversight process?
<--- Score

61. Which Market insights leaders data should be retained?
<--- Score

62. How often will data be collected for measures?
<--- Score

63. What kind of crime could a potential new hire have committed that would not only not disqualify him/her from being hired by your organization, but would actually indicate that he/she might be a particularly good fit?
<--- Score

64. Is the final output clearly identified?
<--- Score

65. Who is involved with workflow mapping?
<--- Score

66. Do you have the authority to produce the output?
<--- Score

67. Who is involved in the management review process?
<--- Score

68. What is the Market insights leaders Driver?
<--- Score

69. What is the output?
<--- Score

70. What data is gathered?
<--- Score

71. How is the data gathered?
<--- Score

72. What types of data do your Market insights leaders indicators require?

<--- Score

73. What are the processes for audit reporting and management?
<--- Score

74. How has the Market insights leaders data been gathered?
<--- Score

75. What other organizational variables, such as reward systems or communication systems, affect the performance of this Market insights leaders process?
<--- Score

76. How are outputs preserved and protected?
<--- Score

77. Identify an operational issue in your organization, for example, could a particular task be done more quickly or more efficiently by Market insights leaders?
<--- Score

78. A compounding model resolution with available relevant data can often provide insight towards a solution methodology; which Market insights leaders models, tools and techniques are necessary?
<--- Score

79. Is there a strict change management process?
<--- Score

80. How do you measure the operational performance of your key work systems and processes, including productivity, cycle time, and other appropriate

measures of process effectiveness, efficiency, and innovation?

<--- Score

81. What qualifications are needed?

<--- Score

82. Was a detailed process map created to amplify critical steps of the 'as is' stakeholder process?

<--- Score

83. Is the required Market insights leaders data gathered?

<--- Score

84. What are your key performance measures or indicators and in-process measures for the control and improvement of your Market insights leaders processes?

<--- Score

85. What qualifications do Market insights leaders leaders need?

<--- Score

86. How is the way you as the leader think and process information affecting your organizational culture?

<--- Score

87. Is pre-qualification of suppliers carried out?

<--- Score

88. What data do you need to collect?

<--- Score

89. Record-keeping requirements flow from the

records needed as inputs, outputs, controls and for transformation of a Market insights leaders process, are the records needed as inputs to the Market insights leaders process available?

<--- Score

90. How will the data be checked for quality?

<--- Score

91. What did the team gain from developing a sub-process map?

<--- Score

92. Has an output goal been set?

<--- Score

93. Are all staff in core Market insights leaders subjects Highly Qualified?

<--- Score

94. An organizationally feasible system request is one that considers the mission, goals and objectives of the organization, key questions are: is the Market insights leaders solution request practical and will it solve a problem or take advantage of an opportunity to achieve company goals?

<--- Score

95. What process improvements will be needed?

<--- Score

96. What are the Market insights leaders business drivers?

<--- Score

97. How do your work systems and key work

processes relate to and capitalize on your core competencies?

<--- Score

98. What are your current levels and trends in key measures or indicators of Market insights leaders product and process performance that are important to and directly serve your customers? How do these results compare with the performance of your competitors and other organizations with similar offerings?

<--- Score

99. How do you ensure that the Market insights leaders opportunity is realistic?

<--- Score

100. What information qualified as important?

<--- Score

101. How do you implement and manage your work processes to ensure that they meet design requirements?

<--- Score

102. What will drive Market insights leaders change?

<--- Score

103. Who owns what data?

<--- Score

104. Have you defined which data is gathered how?

<--- Score

105. How will the Market insights leaders data be captured?
<--- Score

106. What are the revised rough estimates of the financial savings/opportunity for Market insights leaders improvements?
<--- Score

107. What, related to, Market insights leaders processes does your organization outsource?
<--- Score

108. What Market insights leaders data should be managed?
<--- Score

109. What output to create?
<--- Score

110. Can you add value to the current Market insights leaders decision-making process (largely qualitative) by incorporating uncertainty modeling (more quantitative)?
<--- Score

111. Think about the functions involved in your Market insights leaders project, what processes flow from these functions?
<--- Score

112. How do you identify specific Market insights leaders investment opportunities and emerging trends?
<--- Score

113. What are your best practices for minimizing Market insights leaders project risk, while demonstrating incremental value and quick wins throughout the Market insights leaders project lifecycle?
<--- Score

114. How is Market insights leaders data gathered?
<--- Score

115. When should a process be art not science?
<--- Score

116. What conclusions were drawn from the team's data collection and analysis? How did the team reach these conclusions?
<--- Score

117. Do you understand your management processes today?
<--- Score

118. Who will facilitate the team and process?
<--- Score

119. Where is Market insights leaders data gathered?
<--- Score

120. How is the Market insights leaders Value Stream Mapping managed?
<--- Score

121. Is the Market insights leaders process severely broken such that a re-design is necessary?
<--- Score

122. Is there an established change management process?
<--- Score

123. Were there any improvement opportunities identified from the process analysis?
<--- Score

124. Were any designed experiments used to generate additional insight into the data analysis?
<--- Score

125. How will the change process be managed?
<--- Score

126. What are the best opportunities for value improvement?
<--- Score

127. What methods do you use to gather Market insights leaders data?
<--- Score

128. What is your organizations process which leads to recognition of value generation?
<--- Score

129. Is the performance gap determined?
<--- Score

130. What are your outputs?
<--- Score

131. What Market insights leaders data do you gather or use now?
<--- Score

132. What is the cost of poor quality as supported by the team's analysis?
<--- Score

133. Are your outputs consistent?
<--- Score

134. Is the suppliers process defined and controlled?
<--- Score

Add up total points for this section:
_ _ _ _ _ = Total points for this section

Divided by: _ _ _ _ _ _ (number of statements answered) = _ _ _ _ _ _
Average score for this section

Transfer your score to the Market insights leaders Index at the beginning of the Self-Assessment.

CRITERION #5: IMPROVE:

INTENT: Develop a practical solution. Innovate, establish and test the solution and to measure the results.

In my belief, the answer to this question is clearly defined:

5 Strongly Agree

4 Agree

3 Neutral

2 Disagree

1 Strongly Disagree

1. What risks do you need to manage?
<--- Score

2. What resources are required for the improvement efforts?
<--- Score

3. Are you assessing Market insights leaders and risk?

<--- Score

4. How do you measure progress and evaluate training effectiveness?
<--- Score

5. What tools were most useful during the improve phase?
<--- Score

6. Is there a high likelihood that any recommendations will achieve their intended results?
<--- Score

7. How does your organization evaluate strategic Market insights leaders success?
<--- Score

8. To what extent does management recognize Market insights leaders as a tool to increase the results?
<--- Score

9. What is Market insights leaders's impact on utilizing the best solution(s)?
<--- Score

10. Is the Market insights leaders documentation thorough?
<--- Score

11. Can you identify any significant risks or exposures to Market insights leaders third- parties (vendors, service providers, alliance partners etc) that concern you?
<--- Score

12. What area needs the greatest improvement?
<--- Score

13. How do you measure risk?
<--- Score

14. Are the risks fully understood, reasonable and manageable?
<--- Score

15. What assumptions are made about the solution and approach?
<--- Score

16. What strategies for Market insights leaders improvement are successful?
<--- Score

17. Will the controls trigger any other risks?
<--- Score

18. How do you improve Market insights leaders service perception, and satisfaction?
<--- Score

19. Which Market insights leaders solution is appropriate?
<--- Score

20. Who will be using the results of the measurement activities?
<--- Score

21. Is the measure of success for Market insights leaders understandable to a variety of people?

<--- Score

22. What criteria will you use to assess your Market insights leaders risks?
<--- Score

23. What is the magnitude of the improvements?
<--- Score

24. What is the team's contingency plan for potential problems occurring in implementation?
<--- Score

25. Who are the people involved in developing and implementing Market insights leaders?
<--- Score

26. Who do you report Market insights leaders results to?
<--- Score

27. What is the implementation plan?
<--- Score

28. What is the risk?
<--- Score

29. Can the solution be designed and implemented within an acceptable time period?
<--- Score

30. Do those selected for the Market insights leaders team have a good general understanding of what Market insights leaders is all about?
<--- Score

31. Is the Market insights leaders risk managed?
<--- Score

32. Who are the Market insights leaders decision makers?
<--- Score

33. How do you decide how much to remunerate an employee?
<--- Score

34. What improvements have been achieved?
<--- Score

35. Is the scope clearly documented?
<--- Score

36. How do you define the solutions' scope?
<--- Score

37. Risk Identification: What are the possible risk events your organization faces in relation to Market insights leaders?
<--- Score

38. Market insights leaders risk decisions: whose call Is It?
<--- Score

39. Are procedures documented for managing Market insights leaders risks?
<--- Score

40. What Market insights leaders improvements can be made?
<--- Score

41. Have you achieved Market insights leaders improvements?
<--- Score

42. Does a good decision guarantee a good outcome?
<--- Score

43. Do you need to do a usability evaluation?
<--- Score

44. Are risk management tasks balanced centrally and locally?
<--- Score

45. Who manages Market insights leaders risk?
<--- Score

46. What are your current levels and trends in key measures or indicators of workforce and leader development?
<--- Score

47. How are policy decisions made and where?
<--- Score

48. Are risk triggers captured?
<--- Score

49. Does the goal represent a desired result that can be measured?
<--- Score

50. Can you integrate quality management and risk management?
<--- Score

51. Is any Market insights leaders documentation required?

<--- Score

52. What are the implications of the one critical Market insights leaders decision 10 minutes, 10 months, and 10 years from now?

<--- Score

53. Is there any other Market insights leaders solution?

<--- Score

54. What can you do to improve?

<--- Score

55. What are the concrete Market insights leaders results?

<--- Score

56. How will you know that you have improved?

<--- Score

57. How can you better manage risk?

<--- Score

58. What were the criteria for evaluating a Market insights leaders pilot?

<--- Score

59. What are the Market insights leaders security risks?

<--- Score

60. Who controls key decisions that will be made?

<--- Score

61. How do you mitigate Market insights leaders risk?

<--- Score

62. How do you keep improving Market insights leaders?

<--- Score

63. What went well, what should change, what can improve?

<--- Score

64. Are decisions made in a timely manner?

<--- Score

65. Where do the Market insights leaders decisions reside?

<--- Score

66. Is supporting Market insights leaders documentation required?

<--- Score

67. How will you know when its improved?

<--- Score

68. Who will be responsible for documenting the Market insights leaders requirements in detail?

<--- Score

69. What should a proof of concept or pilot accomplish?

<--- Score

70. Have you identified breakpoints and/or risk tolerances that will trigger broad consideration of

a potential need for intervention or modification of strategy?
<--- Score

71. Who manages supplier risk management in your organization?
<--- Score

72. How do the Market insights leaders results compare with the performance of your competitors and other organizations with similar offerings?
<--- Score

73. How will you measure the results?
<--- Score

74. In the past few months, what is the smallest change you have made that has had the biggest positive result? What was it about that small change that produced the large return?
<--- Score

75. How do you improve your likelihood of success ?
<--- Score

76. What were the underlying assumptions on the cost-benefit analysis?
<--- Score

77. For estimation problems, how do you develop an estimation statement?
<--- Score

78. Where do you need Market insights leaders improvement?
<--- Score

79. What are the affordable Market insights leaders risks?
<--- Score

80. What tools were used to evaluate the potential solutions?
<--- Score

81. Are events managed to resolution?
<--- Score

82. What practices helps your organization to develop its capacity to recognize patterns?
<--- Score

83. How do you manage Market insights leaders risk?
<--- Score

84. Do you combine technical expertise with business knowledge and Market insights leaders Key topics include lifecycles, development approaches, requirements and how to make a business case?
<--- Score

85. Is risk periodically assessed?
<--- Score

86. How do you deal with Market insights leaders risk?
<--- Score

87. How will you recognize and celebrate results?
<--- Score

88. Do you have the optimal project management team structure?

<--- Score

89. How can skill-level changes improve Market insights leaders?

<--- Score

90. What tools were used to tap into the creativity and encourage 'outside the box' thinking?

<--- Score

91. Who will be responsible for making the decisions to include or exclude requested changes once Market insights leaders is underway?

<--- Score

92. How do you go about comparing Market insights leaders approaches/solutions?

<--- Score

93. How can you improve Market insights leaders?

<--- Score

94. What alternative responses are available to manage risk?

<--- Score

95. What lessons, if any, from a pilot were incorporated into the design of the full-scale solution?

<--- Score

96. At what point will vulnerability assessments be performed once Market insights leaders is put into production (e.g., ongoing Risk Management after implementation)?

<--- Score

97. Would you develop a Market insights leaders Communication Strategy?
<--- Score

98. How do you measure improved Market insights leaders service perception, and satisfaction?
<--- Score

99. What to do with the results or outcomes of measurements?
<--- Score

100. Who controls the risk?
<--- Score

101. What is the Market insights leaders's sustainability risk?
<--- Score

102. What tools do you use once you have decided on a Market insights leaders strategy and more importantly how do you choose?
<--- Score

103. What needs improvement? Why?
<--- Score

104. What actually has to improve and by how much?
<--- Score

105. Do vendor agreements bring new compliance risk ?
<--- Score

106. How can the phases of Market insights leaders development be identified?
<--- Score

107. How risky is your organization?
<--- Score

108. Which of the recognised risks out of all risks can be most likely transferred?
<--- Score

109. What error proofing will be done to address some of the discrepancies observed in the 'as is' process?
<--- Score

110. Who are the key stakeholders for the Market insights leaders evaluation?
<--- Score

111. How will you know that a change is an improvement?
<--- Score

112. How scalable is your Market insights leaders solution?
<--- Score

113. Explorations of the frontiers of Market insights leaders will help you build influence, improve Market insights leaders, optimize decision making, and sustain change, what is your approach?
<--- Score

114. Was a Market insights leaders charter developed?

<--- Score

115. How are Market insights leaders risks managed?
<--- Score

116. When you map the key players in your own work and the types/domains of relationships with them, which relationships do you find easy and which challenging, and why?
<--- Score

117. Is the solution technically practical?
<--- Score

118. Who makes the Market insights leaders decisions in your organization?
<--- Score

119. For decision problems, how do you develop a decision statement?
<--- Score

120. Do you cover the five essential competencies: Communication, Collaboration,Innovation, Adaptability, and Leadership that improve an organizations ability to leverage the new Market insights leaders in a volatile global economy?
<--- Score

121. Is Market insights leaders documentation maintained?
<--- Score

122. How do you link measurement and risk?
<--- Score

123. How can you improve performance?
<--- Score

124. Who should make the Market insights leaders decisions?
<--- Score

125. What do you want to improve?
<--- Score

126. How is continuous improvement applied to risk management?
<--- Score

127. Risk factors: what are the characteristics of Market insights leaders that make it risky?
<--- Score

128. How is knowledge sharing about risk management improved?
<--- Score

129. How do you manage and improve your Market insights leaders work systems to deliver customer value and achieve organizational success and sustainability?
<--- Score

130. If you could go back in time five years, what decision would you make differently? What is your best guess as to what decision you're making today you might regret five years from now?
<--- Score

Add up total points for this section:
_ _ _ _ _ = Total points for this section

Divided by: _____ (number of
statements answered) = _____
Average score for this section

Transfer your score to the Market
insights leaders Index at the beginning
of the Self-Assessment.

CRITERION #6: CONTROL:

INTENT: Implement the practical solution. Maintain the performance and correct possible complications.

In my belief, the answer to this question is clearly defined:

5 Strongly Agree

4 Agree

3 Neutral

2 Disagree

1 Strongly Disagree

1. What are the known security controls?
<--- Score

2. What are customers monitoring?
<--- Score

3. Will any special training be provided for results interpretation?
<--- Score

4. Have new or revised work instructions resulted?
<--- Score

5. Does job training on the documented procedures need to be part of the process team's education and training?
<--- Score

6. Are the Market insights leaders standards challenging?
<--- Score

7. Is a response plan in place for when the input, process, or output measures indicate an 'out-of-control' condition?
<--- Score

8. Is the Market insights leaders test/monitoring cost justified?
<--- Score

9. Is reporting being used or needed?
<--- Score

10. Is new knowledge gained imbedded in the response plan?
<--- Score

11. You may have created your quality measures at a time when you lacked resources, technology wasn't up to the required standard, or low service levels were the industry norm. Have those circumstances changed?
<--- Score

12. What quality tools were useful in the control phase?
<--- Score

13. Are pertinent alerts monitored, analyzed and distributed to appropriate personnel?
<--- Score

14. Will the team be available to assist members in planning investigations?
<--- Score

15. How likely is the current Market insights leaders plan to come in on schedule or on budget?
<--- Score

16. Will your goals reflect your program budget?
<--- Score

17. How will the day-to-day responsibilities for monitoring and continual improvement be transferred from the improvement team to the process owner?
<--- Score

18. Can you adapt and adjust to changing Market insights leaders situations?
<--- Score

19. What should the next improvement project be that is related to Market insights leaders?
<--- Score

20. How do senior leaders actions reflect a commitment to the organizations Market insights leaders values?

<--- Score

21. How do you establish and deploy modified action plans if circumstances require a shift in plans and rapid execution of new plans?
<--- Score

22. Do the viable solutions scale to future needs?
<--- Score

23. How do you select, collect, align, and integrate Market insights leaders data and information for tracking daily operations and overall organizational performance, including progress relative to strategic objectives and action plans?
<--- Score

24. What do your reports reflect?
<--- Score

25. Are there documented procedures?
<--- Score

26. In the case of a Market insights leaders project, the criteria for the audit derive from implementation objectives, an audit of a Market insights leaders project involves assessing whether the recommendations outlined for implementation have been met, can you track that any Market insights leaders project is implemented as planned, and is it working?
<--- Score

27. What do you measure to verify effectiveness gains?
<--- Score

28. How do you monitor usage and cost?
<--- Score

29. How will report readings be checked to effectively monitor performance?
<--- Score

30. Who sets the Market insights leaders standards?
<--- Score

31. How will the process owner verify improvement in present and future sigma levels, process capabilities?
<--- Score

32. Do you monitor the Market insights leaders decisions made and fine tune them as they evolve?
<--- Score

33. What is the best design framework for Market insights leaders organization now that, in a post industrial-age if the top-down, command and control model is no longer relevant?
<--- Score

34. How can you best use all of your knowledge repositories to enhance learning and sharing?
<--- Score

35. Are suggested corrective/restorative actions indicated on the response plan for known causes to problems that might surface?
<--- Score

36. What are the performance and scale of the Market insights leaders tools?

<--- Score

37. What other systems, operations, processes, and infrastructures (hiring practices, staffing, training, incentives/rewards, metrics/dashboards/scorecards, etc.) need updates, additions, changes, or deletions in order to facilitate knowledge transfer and improvements?
<--- Score

38. Who will be in control?
<--- Score

39. How will you measure your QA plan's effectiveness?
<--- Score

40. How will Market insights leaders decisions be made and monitored?
<--- Score

41. Does the response plan contain a definite closed loop continual improvement scheme (e.g., plan-do-check-act)?
<--- Score

42. What is your plan to assess your security risks?
<--- Score

43. How will input, process, and output variables be checked to detect for sub-optimal conditions?
<--- Score

44. Is there a control plan in place for sustaining improvements (short and long-term)?
<--- Score

45. Is there a Market insights leaders Communication plan covering who needs to get what information when?
<--- Score

46. Has the improved process and its steps been standardized?
<--- Score

47. Does a troubleshooting guide exist or is it needed?
<--- Score

48. Does the Market insights leaders performance meet the customer's requirements?
<--- Score

49. Do you monitor the effectiveness of your Market insights leaders activities?
<--- Score

50. What is the control/monitoring plan?
<--- Score

51. Are documented procedures clear and easy to follow for the operators?
<--- Score

52. What should you measure to verify efficiency gains?
<--- Score

53. How do you encourage people to take control and responsibility?
<--- Score

54. Where do ideas that reach policy makers and planners as proposals for Market insights leaders strengthening and reform actually originate?
<--- Score

55. Are controls in place and consistently applied?
<--- Score

56. Is there documentation that will support the successful operation of the improvement?
<--- Score

57. Are new process steps, standards, and documentation ingrained into normal operations?
<--- Score

58. How is change control managed?
<--- Score

59. Do the Market insights leaders decisions you make today help people and the planet tomorrow?
<--- Score

60. Who is the Market insights leaders process owner?
<--- Score

61. Who is going to spread your message?
<--- Score

62. Can support from partners be adjusted?
<--- Score

63. What other areas of the group might benefit from the Market insights leaders team's improvements, knowledge, and learning?
<--- Score

64. What key inputs and outputs are being measured on an ongoing basis?
<--- Score

65. Who has control over resources?
<--- Score

66. Implementation Planning: is a pilot needed to test the changes before a full roll out occurs?
<--- Score

67. Is there a transfer of ownership and knowledge to process owner and process team tasked with the responsibilities.
<--- Score

68. Against what alternative is success being measured?
<--- Score

69. Is a response plan established and deployed?
<--- Score

70. What do you stand for--and what are you against?
<--- Score

71. What is the standard for acceptable Market insights leaders performance?
<--- Score

72. What can you control?
<--- Score

73. How do your controls stack up?
<--- Score

74. Are the planned controls in place?
<--- Score

75. Is there a recommended audit plan for routine surveillance inspections of Market insights leaders's gains?
<--- Score

76. How do controls support value?
<--- Score

77. What are your results for key measures or indicators of the accomplishment of your Market insights leaders strategy and action plans, including building and strengthening core competencies?
<--- Score

78. Is knowledge gained on process shared and institutionalized?
<--- Score

79. How will the process owner and team be able to hold the gains?
<--- Score

80. What are the key elements of your Market insights leaders performance improvement system, including your evaluation, organizational learning, and innovation processes?
<--- Score

81. How do you spread information?
<--- Score

82. How is Market insights leaders project cost

planned, managed, monitored?
<--- Score

83. How might the group capture best practices and lessons learned so as to leverage improvements?
<--- Score

84. What are the critical parameters to watch?
<--- Score

85. What is the recommended frequency of auditing?
<--- Score

86. Is there a standardized process?
<--- Score

87. What Market insights leaders standards are applicable?
<--- Score

88. What adjustments to the strategies are needed?
<--- Score

89. Are operating procedures consistent?
<--- Score

90. Is there an action plan in case of emergencies?
<--- Score

91. How will new or emerging customer needs/ requirements be checked/communicated to orient the process toward meeting the new specifications and continually reducing variation?
<--- Score

92. Who controls critical resources?

<--- Score

93. Has the Market insights leaders value of standards been quantified?
<--- Score

94. What is your theory of human motivation, and how does your compensation plan fit with that view?
<--- Score

95. Does Market insights leaders appropriately measure and monitor risk?
<--- Score

96. Is there a documented and implemented monitoring plan?
<--- Score

97. Will existing staff require re-training, for example, to learn new business processes?
<--- Score

98. How do you plan for the cost of succession?
<--- Score

Add up total points for this section:
_ _ _ _ _ = Total points for this section

Divided by: _ _ _ _ _ _ (number of statements answered) = _ _ _ _ _ _
Average score for this section

Transfer your score to the Market insights leaders Index at the beginning of the Self-Assessment.

CRITERION #7: SUSTAIN:

INTENT: Retain the benefits.

In my belief, the answer to this question is clearly defined:

5 Strongly Agree

4 Agree

3 Neutral

2 Disagree

1 Strongly Disagree

1. Will it be accepted by users?
<--- Score

2. What is a feasible sequencing of reform initiatives over time?
<--- Score

3. How do you foster innovation?
<--- Score

4. Is the Market insights leaders organization

completing tasks effectively and efficiently?
<--- Score

5. Who are four people whose careers you have enhanced?
<--- Score

6. Did your employees make progress today?
<--- Score

7. Who, on the executive team or the board, has spoken to a customer recently?
<--- Score

8. What trouble can you get into?
<--- Score

9. What is the source of the strategies for Market insights leaders strengthening and reform?
<--- Score

10. What are the rules and assumptions your industry operates under? What if the opposite were true?
<--- Score

11. Have benefits been optimized with all key stakeholders?
<--- Score

12. Are you using a design thinking approach and integrating Innovation, Market insights leaders Experience, and Brand Value?
<--- Score

13. Who have you, as a company, historically been when you've been at your best?

<--- Score

14. What could happen if you do not do it?
<--- Score

15. What is your competitive advantage?
<--- Score

16. What have you done to protect your business from competitive encroachment?
<--- Score

17. Which Market insights leaders goals are the most important?
<--- Score

18. What happens when a new employee joins the organization?
<--- Score

19. How can you become the company that would put you out of business?
<--- Score

20. How can you become more high-tech but still be high touch?
<--- Score

21. What are the key enablers to make this Market insights leaders move?
<--- Score

22. Is your strategy driving your strategy? Or is the way in which you allocate resources driving your strategy?
<--- Score

23. Do you think you know, or do you know you know ?

<--- Score

24. Have new benefits been realized?

<--- Score

25. Are your responses positive or negative?

<--- Score

26. What new services of functionality will be implemented next with Market insights leaders ?

<--- Score

27. Are you satisfied with your current role? If not, what is missing from it?

<--- Score

28. What is your BATNA (best alternative to a negotiated agreement)?

<--- Score

29. Do you feel that more should be done in the Market insights leaders area?

<--- Score

30. What is an unauthorized commitment?

<--- Score

31. Do you have the right capabilities and capacities?

<--- Score

32. Which functions and people interact with the supplier and or customer?

<--- Score

33. If you got fired and a new hire took your place, what would she do different?
<--- Score

34. How will you insure seamless interoperability of Market insights leaders moving forward?
<--- Score

35. What must you excel at?
<--- Score

36. Is Market insights leaders dependent on the successful delivery of a current project?
<--- Score

37. What have been your experiences in defining long range Market insights leaders goals?
<--- Score

38. What information is critical to your organization that your executives are ignoring?
<--- Score

39. How are you doing compared to your industry?
<--- Score

40. Why will customers want to buy your organizations products/services?
<--- Score

41. What relationships among Market insights leaders trends do you perceive?
<--- Score

42. What are the barriers to increased Market insights leaders production?
<--- Score

43. What are your personal philosophies regarding Market insights leaders and how do they influence your work?
<--- Score

44. Whose voice (department, ethnic group, women, older workers, etc) might you have missed hearing from in your company, and how might you amplify this voice to create positive momentum for your business?
<--- Score

45. In the past year, what have you done (or could you have done) to increase the accurate perception of your company/brand as ethical and honest?
<--- Score

46. How much does Market insights leaders help?
<--- Score

47. What trophy do you want on your mantle?
<--- Score

48. How can you negotiate Market insights leaders successfully with a stubborn boss, an irate client, or a deceitful coworker?
<--- Score

49. Will there be any necessary staff changes (redundancies or new hires)?
<--- Score

50. What are you trying to prove to yourself, and how might it be hijacking your life and business success?

<--- Score

51. What is effective Market insights leaders?

<--- Score

52. What stupid rule would you most like to kill?

<--- Score

53. How do you listen to customers to obtain actionable information?

<--- Score

54. Is your basic point _____ or _____?

<--- Score

55. Are you changing as fast as the world around you?

<--- Score

56. Do you know what you are doing? And who do you call if you don't?

<--- Score

57. What Market insights leaders modifications can you make work for you?

<--- Score

58. How do you determine the key elements that affect Market insights leaders workforce satisfaction, how are these elements determined for different workforce groups and segments?

<--- Score

59. How much contingency will be available in the

budget?
<--- Score

60. How can you incorporate support to ensure safe and effective use of Market insights leaders into the services that you provide?
<--- Score

61. How do you make it meaningful in connecting Market insights leaders with what users do day-to-day?
<--- Score

62. What are current Market insights leaders paradigms?
<--- Score

63. What threat is Market insights leaders addressing?
<--- Score

64. What did you miss in the interview for the worst hire you ever made?
<--- Score

65. Who are your customers?
<--- Score

66. Operational - will it work?
<--- Score

67. What is the estimated value of the project?
<--- Score

68. What is the range of capabilities?
<--- Score

69. How is implementation research currently incorporated into each of your goals?
<--- Score

70. What you are going to do to affect the numbers?
<--- Score

71. How do you engage the workforce, in addition to satisfying them?
<--- Score

72. Are you maintaining a past–present–future perspective throughout the Market insights leaders discussion?
<--- Score

73. What projects are going on in the organization today, and what resources are those projects using from the resource pools?
<--- Score

74. Why is Market insights leaders important for you now?
<--- Score

75. If your company went out of business tomorrow, would anyone who doesn't get a paycheck here care?
<--- Score

76. Are new benefits received and understood?
<--- Score

77. How long will it take to change?
<--- Score

78. What is the recommended frequency of auditing?

<--- Score

79. Can you break it down?

<--- Score

80. What is the big Market insights leaders idea?

<--- Score

81. How do you ensure that implementations of Market insights leaders products are done in a way that ensures safety?

<--- Score

82. Can you maintain your growth without detracting from the factors that have contributed to your success?

<--- Score

83. What happens at your organization when people fail?

<--- Score

84. How do you proactively clarify deliverables and Market insights leaders quality expectations?

<--- Score

85. What are the essentials of internal Market insights leaders management?

<--- Score

86. Ask yourself: how would you do this work if you only had one staff member to do it?

<--- Score

87. Do you have an implicit bias for capital investments over people investments?
<--- Score

88. Are you relevant? Will you be relevant five years from now? Ten?
<--- Score

89. Which models, tools and techniques are necessary?
<--- Score

90. What are you challenging?
<--- Score

91. Who uses your product in ways you never expected?
<--- Score

92. What role does communication play in the success or failure of a Market insights leaders project?
<--- Score

93. What may be the consequences for the performance of an organization if all stakeholders are not consulted regarding Market insights leaders?
<--- Score

94. How do you keep the momentum going?
<--- Score

95. What are the success criteria that will indicate that Market insights leaders objectives have been met and the benefits delivered?
<--- Score

96. How do you maintain Market insights leaders's Integrity?
<--- Score

97. Do you have the right people on the bus?
<--- Score

98. How do you lead with Market insights leaders in mind?
<--- Score

99. Is there any existing Market insights leaders governance structure?
<--- Score

100. How do you keep records, of what?
<--- Score

101. What are strategies for increasing support and reducing opposition?
<--- Score

102. How do you go about securing Market insights leaders?
<--- Score

103. How do you foster the skills, knowledge, talents, attributes, and characteristics you want to have?
<--- Score

104. How do you provide a safe environment -physically and emotionally?
<--- Score

105. Who is the main stakeholder, with ultimate responsibility for driving Market insights leaders

forward?
<--- Score

106. What is the craziest thing you can do?
<--- Score

107. What business benefits will Market insights leaders goals deliver if achieved?
<--- Score

108. Has implementation been effective in reaching specified objectives so far?
<--- Score

109. Think of your Market insights leaders project, what are the main functions?
<--- Score

110. What happens if you do not have enough funding?
<--- Score

111. What one word do you want to own in the minds of your customers, employees, and partners?
<--- Score

112. What are specific Market insights leaders rules to follow?
<--- Score

113. Why do and why don't your customers like your organization?
<--- Score

114. In retrospect, of the projects that you pulled the plug on, what percent do you wish had been allowed

to keep going, and what percent do you wish had ended earlier?

<--- Score

115. What is your formula for success in Market insights leaders ?

<--- Score

116. Do you have past Market insights leaders successes?

<--- Score

117. Is Market insights leaders realistic, or are you setting yourself up for failure?

<--- Score

118. Who else should you help?

<--- Score

119. Are assumptions made in Market insights leaders stated explicitly?

<--- Score

120. In a project to restructure Market insights leaders outcomes, which stakeholders would you involve?

<--- Score

121. Do you think Market insights leaders accomplishes the goals you expect it to accomplish?

<--- Score

122. If you were responsible for initiating and implementing major changes in your organization, what steps might you take to ensure acceptance of those changes?

<--- Score

123. Who is responsible for Market insights leaders?
<--- Score

124. What is your Market insights leaders strategy?
<--- Score

125. How important is Market insights leaders to the user organizations mission?
<--- Score

126. Who will be responsible for deciding whether Market insights leaders goes ahead or not after the initial investigations?
<--- Score

127. If your customer were your grandmother, would you tell her to buy what you're selling?
<--- Score

128. Do Market insights leaders rules make a reasonable demand on a users capabilities?
<--- Score

129. How do you manage Market insights leaders Knowledge Management (KM)?
<--- Score

130. What is the purpose of Market insights leaders in relation to the mission?
<--- Score

131. What would you recommend your friend do if he/she were facing this dilemma?
<--- Score

132. How likely is it that a customer would recommend your company to a friend or colleague?
<--- Score

133. Are there any activities that you can take off your to do list?
<--- Score

134. Who do we want your customers to become?
<--- Score

135. Do you say no to customers for no reason?
<--- Score

136. How do you govern and fulfill your societal responsibilities?
<--- Score

137. Why should people listen to you?
<--- Score

138. Who do you think the world wants your organization to be?
<--- Score

139. If you had to leave your organization for a year and the only communication you could have with employees/colleagues was a single paragraph, what would you write?
<--- Score

140. How do you set Market insights leaders stretch targets and how do you get people to not only participate in setting these stretch targets but also that they strive to achieve these?
<--- Score

141. What unique value proposition (UVP) do you offer?

<--- Score

142. What are the business goals Market insights leaders is aiming to achieve?

<--- Score

143. If there were zero limitations, what would you do differently?

<--- Score

144. How do you stay inspired?

<--- Score

145. How will you motivate the stakeholders with the least vested interest?

<--- Score

146. Which individuals, teams or departments will be involved in Market insights leaders?

<--- Score

147. How do you cross-sell and up-sell your Market insights leaders success?

<--- Score

148. What is it like to work for you?

<--- Score

149. What goals did you miss?

<--- Score

150. What counts that you are not counting?

<--- Score

151. What do we do when new problems arise?
<--- Score

152. Do you know who is a friend or a foe?
<--- Score

153. What is the overall business strategy?
<--- Score

154. What are internal and external Market insights leaders relations?
<--- Score

155. Who is responsible for errors?
<--- Score

156. Political -is anyone trying to undermine this project?
<--- Score

157. Would you rather sell to knowledgeable and informed customers or to uninformed customers?
<--- Score

158. When information truly is ubiquitous, when reach and connectivity are completely global, when computing resources are infinite, and when a whole new set of impossibilities are not only possible, but happening, what will that do to your business?
<--- Score

159. Why should you adopt a Market insights leaders framework?
<--- Score

160. How do customers see your organization?
<--- Score

161. Do you have enough freaky customers in your portfolio pushing you to the limit day in and day out?
<--- Score

162. Why is it important to have senior management support for a Market insights leaders project?
<--- Score

163. What is your question? Why?
<--- Score

164. What should you stop doing?
<--- Score

165. What are the usability implications of Market insights leaders actions?
<--- Score

166. What would have to be true for the option on the table to be the best possible choice?
<--- Score

167. Marketing budgets are tighter, consumers are more skeptical, and social media has changed forever the way we talk about Market insights leaders, how do you gain traction?
<--- Score

168. What are the top 3 things at the forefront of your Market insights leaders agendas for the next 3 years?
<--- Score

169. What potential megatrends could make your

business model obsolete?

<--- Score

170. What does your signature ensure?

<--- Score

171. Why not do Market insights leaders?

<--- Score

172. Who do you want your customers to become?

<--- Score

173. What are your most important goals for the strategic Market insights leaders objectives?

<--- Score

174. How will you ensure you get what you expected?

<--- Score

175. What was the last experiment you ran?

<--- Score

176. Who is responsible for ensuring appropriate resources (time, people and money) are allocated to Market insights leaders?

<--- Score

177. Are the criteria for selecting recommendations stated?

<--- Score

178. What are the short and long-term Market insights leaders goals?

<--- Score

179. Is there any reason to believe the opposite of

my current belief?
<--- Score

180. What management system can you use to leverage the Market insights leaders experience, ideas, and concerns of the people closest to the work to be done?
<--- Score

181. How do you deal with Market insights leaders changes?
<--- Score

182. If you had to rebuild your organization without any traditional competitive advantages (i.e., no killer technology, promising research, innovative product/service delivery model, etcetera), how would your people have to approach their work and collaborate together in order to create the necessary conditions for success?
<--- Score

183. How do you track customer value, profitability or financial return, organizational success, and sustainability?
<--- Score

184. What is something you believe that nearly no one agrees with you on?
<--- Score

185. What are the challenges?
<--- Score

186. Are the assumptions believable and achievable?

<--- Score

187. What will be the consequences to the stakeholder (financial, reputation etc) if Market insights leaders does not go ahead or fails to deliver the objectives?
<--- Score

188. Who will manage the integration of tools?
<--- Score

189. If you find that you havent accomplished one of the goals for one of the steps of the Market insights leaders strategy, what will you do to fix it?
<--- Score

190. Where can you break convention?
<--- Score

191. Is there a work around that you can use?
<--- Score

192. What are the potential basics of Market insights leaders fraud?
<--- Score

193. Is the impact that Market insights leaders has shown?
<--- Score

194. Who will determine interim and final deadlines?
<--- Score

195. At what moment would you think; Will I get fired?
<--- Score

196. Who are the key stakeholders?
<--- Score

197. Were lessons learned captured and communicated?
<--- Score

198. Is it economical; do you have the time and money?
<--- Score

199. What are the gaps in your knowledge and experience?
<--- Score

200. How will you know that the Market insights leaders project has been successful?
<--- Score

201. Do you see more potential in people than they do in themselves?
<--- Score

202. What knowledge, skills and characteristics mark a good Market insights leaders project manager?
<--- Score

203. Are you making progress, and are you making progress as Market insights leaders leaders?
<--- Score

204. What is the funding source for this project?
<--- Score

205. What Market insights leaders skills are most important?

<--- Score

206. Who is on the team?
<--- Score

207. How does Market insights leaders integrate with other stakeholder initiatives?
<--- Score

208. How do you transition from the baseline to the target?
<--- Score

209. Is a Market insights leaders team work effort in place?
<--- Score

210. Can the schedule be done in the given time?
<--- Score

211. Are all key stakeholders present at all Structured Walkthroughs?
<--- Score

212. Instead of going to current contacts for new ideas, what if you reconnected with dormant contacts--the people you used to know? If you were going reactivate a dormant tie, who would it be?
<--- Score

213. Can you do all this work?
<--- Score

Add up total points for this section:
_ _ _ _ _ = Total points for this section

Divided by: _____ (number of
statements answered) = _____
Average score for this section

Transfer your score to the Market
insights leaders Index at the beginning
of the Self-Assessment.

Market Insights Leaders and Managing Projects, Criteria for Project Managers:

1.0 Initiating Process Group: Market Insights Leaders

1. What do you need to do?

2. During which stage of Risk planning are modeling techniques used to determine overall effects of risks on Market Insights Leaders project objectives for high probability, high impact risks?

3. Mitigate. what will you do to minimize the impact should the risk event occur?

4. Who is performing the work of the Market Insights Leaders project?

5. Do you know the roles & responsibilities required for this Market Insights Leaders project?

6. What communication items need improvement?

7. The Market Insights Leaders project you are managing has nine stakeholders. How many channel of communications are there between corresponding stakeholders?

8. What were things that you did well, and could improve, and how?

9. Do you understand the communication expectations for this Market Insights Leaders project?

10. How will you know you did it?

11. Are there resources to maintain and support the

outcome of the Market Insights Leaders project?

12. What are the inputs required to produce the deliverables?

13. Do you understand all business (operational), technical, resource and vendor risks associated with the Market Insights Leaders project?

14. Establishment of pm office?

15. At which stage, in a typical Market Insights Leaders project do stake holders have maximum influence?

16. If action is called for, what form should it take?

17. Who are the Market Insights Leaders project stakeholders?

18. What are the short and long term implications?

19. How well did you do?

20. What business situation is being addressed?

1.1 Project Charter: Market Insights Leaders

21. What are the assigned resources?

22. What goes into your Market Insights Leaders project Charter?

23. What are the known stakeholder requirements?

24. Who are the stakeholders?

25. Avoid costs, improve service, and/ or comply with a mandate?

26. Why have you chosen the aim you have set forth?

27. Are there special technology requirements?

28. What are the deliverables?

29. What are you trying to accomplish?

30. What ideas do you have for initial tests of change (PDSA cycles)?

31. Is it an improvement over existing products?

32. Customer benefits: what customer requirements does this Market Insights Leaders project address?

33. What is the business need?

34. What is the purpose of the Market Insights Leaders project?

35. Who is the sponsor?

36. Fit with other Products Compliments – Cannibalizes?

37. Major high-level milestone targets: what events measure progress?

38. Must Have?

39. Why do you manage integration?

40. Are you building in-house ?

1.2 Stakeholder Register: Market Insights Leaders

41. What opportunities exist to provide communications?

42. How much influence do they have on the Market Insights Leaders project?

43. Who is managing stakeholder engagement?

44. What & Why?

45. How will reports be created?

46. How should employers make voices heard?

47. How big is the gap?

48. What are the major Market Insights Leaders project milestones requiring communications or providing communications opportunities?

49. What is the power of the stakeholder?

50. Is your organization ready for change?

51. Who wants to talk about Security?

1.3 Stakeholder Analysis Matrix: Market Insights Leaders

52. How much do resources cost?

53. Who has the power to influence the outcomes of the work?

54. Sustainable financial backing?

55. Management cover, succession?

56. Who has control over whom?

57. Are you going to weigh the stakeholders?

58. How will the stakeholder directly benefit from the Market Insights Leaders project and how will this affect the stakeholders motivation?

59. Usps (unique selling points)?

60. How do customers express needs?

61. How to involve media?

62. Do the stakeholders goals and expectations support or conflict with the Market Insights Leaders project goals?

63. How affected by the problem(s)?

64. Competitor intentions - various?

65. Lack of competitive strength?

66. How will the Market Insights Leaders project benefit them?

67. What do you Evaluate?

68. What is the stakeholders name, what is function?

69. Who will be affected by the Market Insights Leaders project?

70. What mechanisms are proposed to monitor and measure Market Insights Leaders project performance in terms of social development outcomes?

71. How to measure the achievement of the Immediate Objective?

2.0 Planning Process Group: Market Insights Leaders

72. On which process should team members spend the most time?

73. To what extent have public/private national resources and/or counterparts been mobilized to contribute to the programs objective and produce results and impacts?

74. Professionals want to know what is expected from them; what are the deliverables?

75. What do they need to know about the Market Insights Leaders project?

76. Is the duration of the program sufficient to ensure a cycle that will Market Insights Leaders project the sustainability of the interventions?

77. To what extent do the intervention objectives and strategies of the Market Insights Leaders project respond to your organizations plans?

78. How are it Market Insights Leaders projects different?

79. How well did the chosen processes fit the needs of the Market Insights Leaders project?

80. What is a Software Development Life Cycle (SDLC)?

81. Why do it Market Insights Leaders projects fail?

82. What will you do?

83. To what extent has a PMO contributed to raising the quality of the design of the Market Insights Leaders project?

84. How does activity resource estimation affect activity duration estimation?

85. Are you just doing busywork to pass the time?

86. Have operating capacities been created and/or reinforced in partners?

87. Do the partners have sufficient financial capacity to keep up the benefits produced by the programme?

88. What input will you be required to provide the Market Insights Leaders project team?

89. Who are the Market Insights Leaders project stakeholders?

90. If a risk event occurs, what will you do?

2.1 Project Management Plan: Market Insights Leaders

91. Are cost risk analysis methods applied to develop contingencies for the estimated total Market Insights Leaders project costs?

92. Are the existing and future without-plan conditions reasonable and appropriate?

93. Are alternatives safe, functional, constructible, economical, reasonable and sustainable?

94. How well are you able to manage your risk?

95. Do there need to be organizational changes?

96. What are the constraints?

97. What are the training needs?

98. Was the peer (technical) review of the cost estimates duly coordinated with the cost estimate center of expertise and addressed in the review documentation and certification?

99. Are the proposed Market Insights Leaders project purposes different than a previously authorized Market Insights Leaders project?

100. When is a Market Insights Leaders project management plan created?

101. Are there any client staffing expectations?

102. Are there non-structural buyout or relocation recommendations?

103. Is mitigation authorized or recommended?

104. If the Market Insights Leaders project is complex or scope is specialized, do you have appropriate and/or qualified staff available to perform the tasks?

105. What is the justification?

106. How do you manage time?

107. Who manages integration?

2.2 Scope Management Plan: Market Insights Leaders

108. What are the Quality Assurance overheads?

109. Is there a formal set of procedures supporting Issues Management?

110. Deliverables -are the deliverables tangible and verifiable?

111. Who is doing what for whom?

112. Are you spending the right amount of money for specific tasks?

113. Are tasks tracked by hours?

114. Has the scope management document been updated and distributed to help prevent scope creep?

115. What went wrong?

116. During what part of the PM process is the Market Insights Leaders project scope statement created?

117. Has process improvement efforts been completed before requirements efforts begin?

118. Timeline and milestones?

119. What does the critical path really mean?

120. Are meeting minutes captured and sent out after the meeting?

121. Are corrective actions and variances reported?

122. Can the Market Insights Leaders project team do several activities in parallel?

123. Are there any windfall benefits that would accrue to the Market Insights Leaders project sponsor or other parties?

124. Is there a set of procedures defining the scope, procedures, and deliverables defining quality control?

125. Do Market Insights Leaders project teams & team members report on status / activities / progress?

2.3 Requirements Management Plan: Market Insights Leaders

126. How will the information be distributed?

127. How will requirements be managed?

128. What is a problem?

129. Could inaccurate or incomplete requirements in this Market Insights Leaders project create a serious risk for the business?

130. Is any organizational data being used or stored?

131. Did you use declarative statements?

132. Who is responsible for quantifying the Market Insights Leaders project requirements?

133. Who is responsible for monitoring and tracking the Market Insights Leaders project requirements?

134. How will you communicate scheduled tasks to other team members?

135. Are actual resources expenditures versus planned expenditures acceptable?

136. How knowledgeable is the primary Stakeholder(s) in the proposed application area?

137. Is requirements work dependent on any other

specific Market Insights Leaders project or non-Market Insights Leaders project activities (e.g. funding, approvals, procurement)?

138. Do you really need to write this document at all?

139. If it exists, where is it housed?

140. How will bidders price evaluations be done, by deliverables, phases, or in a big bang?

141. Who will finally present the work or product(s) for acceptance?

142. Do you have price sheets and a methodology for determining the total proposal cost?

143. How will the requirements become prioritized?

144. Will you have access to stakeholders when you need them?

2.4 Requirements Documentation: Market Insights Leaders

145. Are all functions required by the customer included?

146. Basic work/business process; high-level, what is being touched?

147. What will be the integration problems?

148. Where do you define what is a customer, what are the attributes of customer?

149. Who is interacting with the system?

150. What are the attributes of a customer?

151. How linear / iterative is your Requirements Gathering process (or will it be)?

152. Is the origin of the requirement clearly stated?

153. How will requirements be documented and who signs off on them?

154. How much testing do you need to do to prove that your system is safe?

155. What happens when requirements are wrong?

156. Have the benefits identified with the system being identified clearly?

157. What marketing channels do you want to use: e-mail, letter or sms?

158. What is your Elevator Speech?

159. What facilities must be supported by the system?

160. If applicable; are there issues linked with the fact that this is an offshore Market Insights Leaders project?

161. How will they be documented / shared?

162. Do technical resources exist?

163. Can the requirements be checked?

164. Consistency. are there any requirements conflicts?

2.5 Requirements Traceability Matrix: Market Insights Leaders

165. Why use a WBS?

166. How small is small enough?

167. How will it affect the stakeholders personally in career?

168. What is the WBS?

169. Is there a requirements traceability process in place?

170. Describe the process for approving requirements so they can be added to the traceability matrix and Market Insights Leaders project work can be performed. Will the Market Insights Leaders project requirements become approved in writing?

171. Why do you manage scope?

172. Do you have a clear understanding of all subcontracts in place?

173. Will you use a Requirements Traceability Matrix?

174. What percentage of Market Insights Leaders projects are producing traceability matrices between requirements and other work products?

175. How do you manage scope?

176. What are the chronologies, contingencies, consequences, criteria?

2.6 Project Scope Statement: Market Insights Leaders

177. Any new risks introduced or old risks impacted. Are there issues that could affect the existing requirements for the result, service, or product if the scope changes?

178. Why do you need to manage scope?

179. Elements of scope management that deal with concept development ?

180. Does the scope statement still need some clarity?

181. Have you been able to thoroughly document the Market Insights Leaders projects assumptions and constraints?

182. Is the Market Insights Leaders project manager qualified and experienced in Market Insights Leaders project management?

183. Will this process be communicated to the customer and Market Insights Leaders project team?

184. Relevant - ask yourself can you get there; why are you doing this Market Insights Leaders project?

185. What is the product of this Market Insights Leaders project?

186. Change management vs. change leadership -

what is the difference?

187. Has the Market Insights Leaders project scope statement been reviewed as part of the baseline process?

188. What went right?

189. Were potential customers involved early in the planning process?

190. Is there a Change Management Board?

191. Are the meetings set up to have assigned note takers that will add action/issues to the issue list?

192. What is a process you might recommend to verify the accuracy of the research deliverable?

193. Will tasks be marked complete only after QA has been successfully completed?

194. Is the change control process documented and on file?

195. Have you been able to easily identify success criteria and create objective measurements for each of the Market Insights Leaders project scopes goal statements?

2.7 Assumption and Constraint Log: Market Insights Leaders

196. What is positive about the current process?

197. What would you gain if you spent time working to improve this process?

198. What strengths do you have?

199. Does the document/deliverable meet all requirements (for example, statement of work) specific to this deliverable?

200. Do the requirements meet the standards of correctness, completeness, consistency, accuracy, and readability?

201. What other teams / processes would be impacted by changes to the current process, and how?

202. Model-building: what data-analytic strategies are useful when building proportional-hazards models?

203. After observing execution of process, is it in compliance with the documented Plan?

204. Contradictory information between different documents?

205. Are best practices and metrics employed to identify issues, progress, performance, etc.?

206. If it is out of compliance, should the process be amended or should the Plan be amended?

207. Is there adequate stakeholder participation for the vetting of requirements definition, changes and management?

208. Have Market Insights Leaders project management standards and procedures been established and documented?

209. What worked well?

210. Does the plan conform to standards?

211. Are there processes in place to ensure that all the terms and code concepts have been documented consistently?

212. Has a Market Insights Leaders project Communications Plan been developed?

213. Does the traceability documentation describe the tool and/or mechanism to be used to capture traceability throughout the life cycle?

214. When can log be discarded?

2.8 Work Breakdown Structure: Market Insights Leaders

215. What is the probability that the Market Insights Leaders project duration will exceed xx weeks?

216. How big is a work-package?

217. When do you stop?

218. What is the probability of completing the Market Insights Leaders project in less that xx days?

219. Why is it useful?

220. Is the work breakdown structure (wbs) defined and is the scope of the Market Insights Leaders project clear with assigned deliverable owners?

221. How much detail?

222. What has to be done?

223. How many levels?

224. Is it a change in scope?

225. How will you and your Market Insights Leaders project team define the Market Insights Leaders projects scope and work breakdown structure?

226. Do you need another level?

227. How far down?

228. Is it still viable?

229. Who has to do it?

230. When would you develop a Work Breakdown Structure?

231. When does it have to be done?

232. Where does it take place?

2.9 WBS Dictionary: Market Insights Leaders

233. Changes in the direct base to which overhead costs are allocated?

234. Does the scheduling system provide for the identification of work progress against technical and other milestones, and also provide for forecasts of completion dates of scheduled work?

235. Should you include sub-activities?

236. Software specification, development, integration, and testing, licenses ?

237. The already stated responsible for overhead performance control of related costs?

238. Authorization to proceed with all authorized work?

239. What is wrong with this Market Insights Leaders project?

240. Are direct or indirect cost adjustments being accomplished according to accounting procedures acceptable to us?

241. Are procedures established to prevent changes to the contract budget base other than the already stated authorized by contractual action?

242. Are the contractors estimates of costs at completion reconcilable with cost data reported to us?

243. Are retroactive changes to direct costs and indirect costs prohibited except for the correction of errors and routine accounting adjustments?

244. What is the goal?

245. What are you counting on?

246. Does the contractors system provide for accurate cost accumulation and assignment to control accounts in a manner consistent with the budgets using recognized acceptable costing techniques?

247. Are all authorized tasks assigned to identified organizational elements?

248. Does the sum of all work package budgets plus planning packages within control accounts equal the budgets assigned to the already stated control accounts?

249. Changes in the nature of the overhead requirements?

250. Is budgeted cost for work performed calculated in a manner consistent with the way work is planned?

2.10 Schedule Management Plan: Market Insights Leaders

251. Have Market Insights Leaders project management standards and procedures been identified / established and documented?

252. Quality assurance overheads?

253. Are target dates established for each milestone deliverable?

254. Is there a formal set of procedures supporting Stakeholder Management?

255. Is stakeholder involvement adequate?

256. Are the payment terms being followed?

257. Time for overtime?

258. Is your organization certified as a broker of the products/supplies?

259. Is your organization certified as a supplier, wholesaler and/or regular dealer?

260. Have all necessary approvals been obtained?

261. Are multiple estimation methods being employed?

262. Is there general agreement & acceptance of the

current status and progress of the Market Insights Leaders project?

263. What weaknesses do you have?

264. Are internal Market Insights Leaders project status meetings held at reasonable intervals?

265. Are adequate resources provided for the quality assurance function?

266. Have activity relationships and interdependencies within tasks been adequately identified?

267. Is documentation created for communication with the suppliers and Vendors?

268. What date will the task finish?

269. Are procurement deliverables arriving on time and to specification?

2.11 Activity List: Market Insights Leaders

270. How much slack is available in the Market Insights Leaders project?

271. How do you determine the late start (LS) for each activity?

272. Is there anything planned that does not need to be here?

273. What will be performed?

274. What are the critical bottleneck activities?

275. What is the LF and LS for each activity?

276. How detailed should a Market Insights Leaders project get?

277. What did not go as well?

278. When do the individual activities need to start and finish?

279. Who will perform the work?

280. When will the work be performed?

281. How can the Market Insights Leaders project be displayed graphically to better visualize the activities?

282. For other activities, how much delay can be tolerated?

283. What is your organizations history in doing similar activities?

284. In what sequence?

285. The wbs is developed as part of a joint planning session. and how do you know that youhave done this right?

286. What went well?

287. How will it be performed?

288. How should ongoing costs be monitored to try to keep the Market Insights Leaders project within budget?

2.12 Activity Attributes: Market Insights Leaders

289. Can more resources be added?

290. Have you identified the Activity Leveling Priority code value on each activity?

291. Where else does it apply?

292. How difficult will it be to complete specific activities on this Market Insights Leaders project?

293. How many resources do you need to complete the work scope within a limit of X number of days?

294. Is there a trend during the year?

295. Are the required resources available?

296. Activity: what is Missing?

297. Are the required resources available or need to be acquired?

298. How much activity detail is required?

299. Does your organization of the data change its meaning?

300. Have constraints been applied to the start and finish milestones for the phases?

301. Do you feel very comfortable with your prediction?

302. Were there other ways you could have organized the data to achieve similar results?

303. What is missing?

2.13 Milestone List: Market Insights Leaders

304. How soon can the activity finish?

305. How late can each activity be finished and started?

306. It is to be a narrative text providing the crucial aspects of your Market Insights Leaders project proposal answering what, who, how, when and where?

307. Can you derive how soon can the whole Market Insights Leaders project finish?

308. How difficult will it be to do specific activities on this Market Insights Leaders project?

309. Reliability of data, plan predictability?

310. New USPs?

311. Describe the industry you are in and the market growth opportunities. What is the market for your technology, product or service?

312. Loss of key staff?

313. Level of the Innovation?

314. Milestone pages should display the UserID of the person who added the milestone. Does a report or

query exist that provides this audit information?

315. What is the market for your technology, product or service?

316. What background experience, skills, and strengths does the team bring to your organization?

317. Political effects?

318. Identify critical paths (one or more) and which activities are on the critical path?

319. Gaps in capabilities?

320. How soon can the activity start?

321. Which path is the critical path?

2.14 Network Diagram: Market Insights Leaders

322. What controls the start and finish of a job?

323. If a current contract exists, can you provide the vendor name, contract start, and contract expiration date?

324. What to do and When?

325. Where do schedules come from?

326. What are the Major Administrative Issues?

327. What must be completed before an activity can be started?

328. What is the lowest cost to complete this Market Insights Leaders project in xx weeks?

329. Are you on time?

330. Where do you schedule uncertainty time?

331. What activity must be completed immediately before this activity can start?

332. What are the tools?

333. Exercise: what is the probability that the Market Insights Leaders project duration will exceed xx weeks?

334. Why must you schedule milestones, such as reviews, throughout the Market Insights Leaders project?

335. Are the gantt chart and/or network diagram updated periodically and used to assess the overall Market Insights Leaders project timetable?

336. Can you calculate the confidence level?

337. If x is long, what would be the completion time if you break x into two parallel parts of y weeks and z weeks?

338. What job or jobs could run concurrently?

339. What activities must follow this activity?

2.15 Activity Resource Requirements: Market Insights Leaders

340. Are there unresolved issues that need to be addressed?

341. What are constraints that you might find during the Human Resource Planning process?

342. Organizational Applicability?

343. Other support in specific areas?

344. Do you use tools like decomposition and rolling-wave planning to produce the activity list and other outputs?

345. When does monitoring begin?

346. Anything else?

347. How many signatures do you require on a check and does this match what is in your policy and procedures?

348. How do you handle petty cash?

349. What is the Work Plan Standard?

350. Why do you do that?

351. Which logical relationship does the PDM use most often?

2.16 Resource Breakdown Structure: Market Insights Leaders

352. What is the number one predictor of a groups productivity?

353. When do they need the information?

354. What defines a successful Market Insights Leaders project?

355. Who delivers the information?

356. What is Market Insights Leaders project communication management?

357. How can this help you with team building?

358. Which resources should be in the resource pool?

359. Why is this important?

360. Who is allowed to see what data about which resources?

361. How should the information be delivered?

362. Who needs what information?

363. What is the purpose of assigning and documenting responsibility?

364. Changes based on input from stakeholders?

365. What is the difference between % Complete and % work?

366. Who is allowed to perform which functions?

2.17 Activity Duration Estimates: Market Insights Leaders

367. Why is there a growing trend in outsourcing, especially in the government?

368. Based on , if you need to shorten the duration of the Market Insights Leaders project, what activity would you try to shorten?

369. Are team building activities completed to improve team performance?

370. Are Market Insights Leaders project results verified and Market Insights Leaders project documents archived?

371. How can others help Market Insights Leaders project managers understand your organizational context for Market Insights Leaders projects?

372. Why should Market Insights Leaders project managers strive to make jobs look easy?

373. Are activity dependencies identified?

374. What are key inputs and outputs of the software?

375. How difficult will it be to complete specific activities on this Market Insights Leaders project?

376. Do your results resemble a normal distribution?

377. Consider the examples of poor quality in information technology Market Insights Leaders projects presented in the What Went Wrong?

378. If Market Insights Leaders project time and cost are not as important as the number of resources used each month, which is the BEST thing to do?

379. Which is correct?

380. Is the cost performance monitored to identify variances from the plan?

381. What is the difference between using brainstorming and the Delphi technique for risk identification?

382. Given your research into similar classes and the work you think is required for this Market Insights Leaders project, what assumptions, variables, or costs would you change from the information provided above?

383. It under budget or over budget?

384. Are contingency plans created to prepare for risk events to occur?

385. Who will provide inputs for it?

386. Does the case present a realistic scenario?

2.18 Duration Estimating Worksheet: Market Insights Leaders

387. What is cost and Market Insights Leaders project cost management?

388. How can the Market Insights Leaders project be displayed graphically to better visualize the activities?

389. When, then?

390. Is a construction detail attached (to aid in explanation)?

391. What is the total time required to complete the Market Insights Leaders project if no delays occur?

392. What work will be included in the Market Insights Leaders project?

393. Is this operation cost effective?

394. Will the Market Insights Leaders project collaborate with the local community and leverage resources?

395. Do any colleagues have experience with your organization and/or RFPs?

396. Does the Market Insights Leaders project provide innovative ways for stakeholders to overcome obstacles or deliver better outcomes?

397. Science = process: remember the scientific method?

398. What is your role?

399. Can the Market Insights Leaders project be constructed as planned?

400. How should ongoing costs be monitored to try to keep the Market Insights Leaders project within budget?

401. Why estimate time and cost?

402. When does your organization expect to be able to complete it?

403. What questions do you have?

2.19 Project Schedule: Market Insights Leaders

404. How can slack be negative?

405. Activity charts and bar charts are graphical representations of a Market Insights Leaders project schedule ...how do they differ?

406. Are you working on the right risks?

407. What is the purpose of a Market Insights Leaders project schedule?

408. Are key risk mitigation strategies added to the Market Insights Leaders project schedule?

409. Should you have a test for each code module?

410. Are activities connected because logic dictates the order in which others occur?

411. Schedule/cost recovery?

412. It allows the Market Insights Leaders project to be delivered on schedule. How Do you Use Schedules?

413. Market Insights Leaders project work estimates Who is managing the work estimate quality of work tasks in the Market Insights Leaders project schedule?

414. How can you shorten the schedule?

415. Did the Market Insights Leaders project come in on schedule?

416. If you can not fix it, how do you do it differently?

417. Change management required?

418. Is the Market Insights Leaders project schedule available for all Market Insights Leaders project team members to review?

419. To what degree is do you feel the entire team was committed to the Market Insights Leaders project schedule?

420. Are the original Market Insights Leaders project schedule and budget realistic?

2.20 Cost Management Plan: Market Insights Leaders

421. Are all resource assumptions documented?

422. Has Market Insights Leaders project success criteria been defined?

423. What are the nine areas of expertise?

424. Estimating responsibilities – how will the responsibilities for cost estimating be allocated?

425. Has a capability assessment been conducted?

426. Have adequate resources been provided by management to ensure Market Insights Leaders project success?

427. Are mitigation strategies identified?

428. What is an Acceptance Management Process?

429. Is a pmo (Market Insights Leaders project management office) in place and provide oversight to the Market Insights Leaders project?

430. Are any non-compliance issues that exist due to State practices communicated to your organization?

431. Scope of work – What is the scope of work for each of the planned contracts?

432. Is there an on-going process in place to monitor Market Insights Leaders project risks?

433. Have stakeholder accountabilities & responsibilities been clearly defined?

434. Escalation criteria met?

435. Are the results of quality assurance reviews provided to affected groups & individuals?

436. Does the Market Insights Leaders project have a Statement of Work?

437. What would you do differently what did not work?

438. Have reserves been created to address risks?

2.21 Activity Cost Estimates: Market Insights Leaders

439. Can you delete activities or make them inactive?

440. What do you want to know about the stay to know if costs were inappropriately high or low?

441. Are data needed on characteristics of care?

442. Would you hire them again?

443. What defines a successful Market Insights Leaders project?

444. Are cost subtotals needed?

445. Specific - is the objective clear in terms of what, how, when, and where the situation will be changed?

446. Who & what determines the need for contracted services?

447. What are you looking for?

448. What makes a good expected result statement?

449. How difficult will it be to do specific tasks on the Market Insights Leaders project?

450. What is the last item a Market Insights Leaders project manager must do to finalize Market Insights Leaders project close-out?

451. Does the activity use a common approach or business function to deliver its results?

452. How do you manage cost?

453. How do you allocate indirect costs to activities?

454. What is a Market Insights Leaders project Management Plan?

455. Is there anything unique in this Market Insights Leaders projects scope statement that will affect resources?

456. How and when do you enter into Market Insights Leaders project Procurement Management?

457. One way to define activities is to consider how organization employees describe jobs to families and friends. You basically want to know, What do you do?

2.22 Cost Estimating Worksheet: Market Insights Leaders

458. Identify the timeframe necessary to monitor progress and collect data to determine how the selected measure has changed?

459. What will others want?

460. What is the purpose of estimating?

461. Does the Market Insights Leaders project provide innovative ways for stakeholders to overcome obstacles or deliver better outcomes?

462. Is the Market Insights Leaders project responsive to community need?

463. How will the results be shared and to whom?

464. Ask: are others positioned to know, are others credible, and will others cooperate?

465. Is it feasible to establish a control group arrangement?

466. What is the estimated labor cost today based upon this information?

467. Will the Market Insights Leaders project collaborate with the local community and leverage resources?

468. Can a trend be established from historical performance data on the selected measure and are the criteria for using trend analysis or forecasting methods met?

469. Who is best positioned to know and assist in identifying corresponding factors?

470. What happens to any remaining funds not used?

471. What additional Market Insights Leaders project(s) could be initiated as a result of this Market Insights Leaders project?

472. What costs are to be estimated?

473. What can be included?

474. What info is needed?

475. Value pocket identification & quantification what are value pockets?

2.23 Cost Baseline: Market Insights Leaders

476. On time?

477. Have the lessons learned been filed with the Market Insights Leaders project Management Office?

478. Does it impact schedule, cost, quality?

479. What threats might prevent you from getting there?

480. What do you want to measure ?

481. Has the actual cost of the Market Insights Leaders project (or Market Insights Leaders project phase) been tallied and compared to the approved budget?

482. When should cost estimates be developed?

483. How long are you willing to wait before you find out were late?

484. Does the suggested change request represent a desired enhancement to the products functionality?

485. How concrete were original objectives?

486. Eac -estimate at completion, what is the total job expected to cost?

487. Are procedures defined by which the cost

baseline may be changed?

488. How likely is it to go wrong?

489. Review your risk triggers -have your risks changed?

490. Where do changes come from?

491. What deliverables come first?

492. On budget?

493. Why do you manage cost?

2.24 Quality Management Plan: Market Insights Leaders

494. How are people conducting sampling trained?

495. How does your organization ensure the reliability, accuracy, timeliness, security and accessibility of data and information?

496. Who is responsible for approving the qapp?

497. How do you prioritize?

498. How do you decide what information to record?

499. How are changes approved?

500. How does your organization establish and maintain customer relationships?

501. How does your organization manage training and evaluate its effectiveness?

502. How do you decide what information needs to be recorded?

503. How are corresponding standards measured?

504. How are calibration records kept?

505. Show/provide copy of procedures for taking field notes?

506. How are data handled when a test is not run per specification?

507. Is the amount of effort justified by the anticipated value of forming a new process?

508. How do you manage quality?

509. How many Market Insights Leaders project staff does this specific process affect?

510. Are there trends or hot spots?

511. How do you measure?

512. Do you periodically review your data quality system to see that it is up to date and appropriate?

2.25 Quality Metrics: Market Insights Leaders

513. Is quality culture a competitive advantage?

514. When will the Final Guidance will be issued?

515. How do you calculate corresponding metrics?

516. What are your organizations next steps?

517. Did the team meet the Market Insights Leaders project success criteria documented in the Quality Metrics Matrix?

518. Was the overall quality better or worse than previous products?

519. Where did complaints, returns and warranty claims come from?

520. What is the CMS Benchmark?

521. Has risk analysis been adequately reviewed?

522. How should customers provide input?

523. Why is now the time for quality metrics?

524. What documentation is required?

525. Which data do others need in one place to target areas of improvement?

526. Has it met internal or external standards?

527. Is a risk containment plan in place?

528. What is the timeline to meet your goal?

529. Were number of defects identified?

530. How effective are your security tests?

531. How do you communicate results and findings to upper management?

2.26 Process Improvement Plan: Market Insights Leaders

532. What lessons have you learned so far?

533. Does explicit definition of the measures exist?

534. Everyone agrees on what process improvement is, right?

535. Are you making progress on the improvement framework?

536. Where do you want to be?

537. Have storage and access mechanisms and procedures been determined?

538. To elicit goal statements, do you ask a question such as, What do you want to achieve?

539. Are you making progress on the goals?

540. Have the supporting tools been developed or acquired?

541. Where are you now?

542. Are there forms and procedures to collect and record the data?

543. Why do you want to achieve the goal?

544. Has a process guide to collect the data been developed?

545. Who should prepare the process improvement action plan?

546. Does your process ensure quality?

547. The motive is determined by asking, Why do you want to achieve this goal?

2.27 Responsibility Assignment Matrix: Market Insights Leaders

548. Are indirect costs accumulated for comparison with the corresponding budgets?

549. Wbs elements contractually specified for reporting of status (lowest level only)?

550. Do you know how your people are allocated?

551. Actual cost of work performed?

552. Are overhead costs budgets established on a basis consistent with anticipated direct business base?

553. Changes in the overhead pool and/or organization structures?

554. Are control accounts opened and closed based on the start and completion of work contained therein?

555. Which Market Insights Leaders project management knowledge area is least mature?

556. Who is the Market Insights Leaders project Manager?

557. Does the accounting system provide a basis for auditing records of direct costs chargeable to the contract?

558. Where does all this information come from?

559. Are the wbs and organizational levels for application of the Market Insights Leaders projected overhead costs identified?

560. When performing is split among two or more roles, is the work clearly defined so that the efforts are coordinated and the communication is clear?

561. Are the bases and rates for allocating costs from each indirect pool consistently applied?

562. Evaluate the performance of operating organizations?

563. What is the primary purpose of the human resource plan?

564. Budgeted cost for work scheduled?

565. Contemplated overhead expenditure for each period based on the best information currently available?

566. Most people let you know when others re too busy, and are others really too busy?

2.28 Roles and Responsibilities: Market Insights Leaders

567. How well did the Market Insights Leaders project Team understand the expectations of specific roles and responsibilities?

568. What areas would you highlight for changes or improvements?

569. Once the responsibilities are defined for the Market Insights Leaders project, have the deliverables, roles and responsibilities been clearly communicated to every participant?

570. Was the expectation clearly communicated?

571. Are your policies supportive of a culture of quality data?

572. Do you take the time to clearly define roles and responsibilities on Market Insights Leaders project tasks?

573. What should you do now to ensure that you are meeting all expectations of your current position?

574. Influence: what areas of organizational decision making are you able to influence when you do not have authority to make the final decision?

575. Who is responsible for each task?

576. What is working well?

577. To decide whether to use a quality measurement, ask how will you know when it is achieved?

578. What should you do now to prepare for your career 5+ years from now?

579. Who is responsible for implementation activities and where will the functions, roles and responsibilities be defined?

580. Who is involved?

581. Where are you most strong as a supervisor?

582. What areas of supervision are challenging for you?

583. What expectations were met?

584. Attainable / achievable: the goal is attainable; can you actually accomplish the goal?

585. What expectations were NOT met?

2.29 Human Resource Management Plan: Market Insights Leaders

586. Is there a formal process for updating the Market Insights Leaders project baseline?

587. How do you determine what key skills and talents are needed to meet the objectives. Is your organization primarily focused on a specific industry?

588. Is there a Steering Committee in place?

589. Is your organization heading towards expansion, outsourcing of certain talents or making cut-backs to save money?

590. Are governance roles and responsibilities documented?

591. Is there a Quality Management Plan?

592. What talent is needed?

593. Where is your organization headed?

594. What are the Staffing Requirements?

595. Measurable - are the targets measurable?

596. What commitments have been made?

597. How does the proposed individual meet each requirement?

598. Has the schedule been baselined?

599. Alignment to strategic goals & objectives?

600. Has the Market Insights Leaders project scope been baselined?

601. How are superior performers differentiated from average performers?

602. Are all key components of a Quality Assurance Plan present?

2.30 Communications Management Plan: Market Insights Leaders

603. What to know?

604. What data is going to be required?

605. Who to share with?

606. Who were proponents/opponents?

607. Do you feel more overwhelmed by stakeholders?

608. Who needs to know and how much?

609. Are there potential barriers between the team and the stakeholder?

610. Do you ask; can you recommend others for you to talk with about this initiative?

611. What is the political influence?

612. Who have you worked with in past, similar initiatives?

613. How did the term stakeholder originate?

614. What is the stakeholders level of authority?

615. What does the stakeholder need from the team?

616. Who did you turn to if you had questions?

617. Do you feel a register helps?

618. What is Market Insights Leaders project communications management?

619. In your work, how much time is spent on stakeholder identification?

620. Are stakeholders internal or external?

621. Are there too many who have an interest in some aspect of your work?

622. What communications method?

2.31 Risk Management Plan: Market Insights Leaders

623. Do requirements demand the use of new analysis, design, or testing methods?

624. Could others have been better mitigated?

625. For software; are compilers and code generators available and suitable for the product to be built?

626. Why might it be late?

627. Have you worked with the customer in the past?

628. Minimize cost and financial risk?

629. Is Market Insights Leaders project scope stable?

630. Why do you need to manage Market Insights Leaders project Risk?

631. What risks are necessary to achieve success?

632. Monitoring -what factors can you track that will enable you to determine if the risk is becoming more or less likely?

633. Are enough people available?

634. Is the necessary data being captured and is it complete and accurate?

635. Maximize short-term return on investment?

636. Management -what contingency plans do you have if the risk becomes a reality?

637. Can you stabilize dynamic risk factors?

638. How is implementation of risk actions performed?

639. What should be done with non-critical risks?

640. How much risk protection can you afford?

641. What can you do to minimize the impact if it does?

2.32 Risk Register: Market Insights Leaders

642. Preventative actions - planned actions to reduce the likelihood a risk will occur and/or reduce the seriousness should it occur. What should you do now?

643. Financial risk -can your organization afford to undertake the Market Insights Leaders project?

644. What are the major risks facing the Market Insights Leaders project?

645. People risk -are people with appropriate skills available to help complete the Market Insights Leaders project?

646. Are there any gaps in the evidence?

647. Do you require further engagement?

648. What will be done?

649. What are you going to do to limit the Market Insights Leaders projects risk exposure due to the identified risks?

650. What is the appropriate level of risk management for this Market Insights Leaders project?

651. Severity Prediction?

652. Methodology: how will risk management be

performed on this Market Insights Leaders project?

653. What should you do now?

654. How are risks graded?

655. What should you do when?

656. Who is going to do it?

657. What has changed since the last period?

658. How well are risks controlled?

659. Having taken action, how did the responses effect change, and where is the Market Insights Leaders project now?

660. Does the evidence highlight any areas to advance opportunities or foster good relations. If yes what steps will be taken?

661. How are risks identified?

2.33 Probability and Impact Assessment: Market Insights Leaders

662. What are the likely future requirements?

663. Risks should be identified during which phase of Market Insights Leaders project management life cycle?

664. What is the experience (performance, attitude, business ethics, etc.) in the past with contractors?

665. What are its business ethics?

666. Your customers business requirements have suddenly shifted because of a new regulatory statute, what now?

667. What are your data sources?

668. Are formal technical reviews part of this process?

669. Are requirements fully understood by the software engineering team and customers?

670. How do risks change during the Market Insights Leaders projects life cycle?

671. Are some people working on multiple Market Insights Leaders projects?

672. How is the Market Insights Leaders project going to be managed?

673. What will be the likely political environment during the life of the Market Insights Leaders project?

674. Do you have a mechanism for managing change?

675. Risk categorization -which of your categories has more risk than others?

676. What should be the gestation period for the Market Insights Leaders project with specific technology?

677. Are there new risks that mitigation strategies might introduce?

678. Is the technology to be built new to your organization?

679. What things might go wrong?

2.34 Probability and Impact Matrix: Market Insights Leaders

680. Do you know the order of planning yet?

681. What are the probable external agencies to act as Market Insights Leaders project manager?

682. Will there be an increase in the political conservatism?

683. Sensitivity analysis -which risks will have the most impact on the Market Insights Leaders project?

684. Can you avoid altogether some things that might go wrong?

685. What can you use the analyzed risks for?

686. What should you do FIRST?

687. What should be the level of coordination?

688. Who are the owners?

689. What should be the gestation period for the Market Insights Leaders project with this technology?

690. Pay attention to the quality of the plans: is the content complete, or does it seem to be lacking detail?

691. How are risks and risk management perceived in

the Market Insights Leaders project?

692. Are Market Insights Leaders project requirements stable?

693. What is the probability of the risk occurring?

694. What do you expect?

695. Can it be changed quickly?

696. How will the consumption pattern change?

697. What new technologies are being explored in the same area?

698. Risk may be made during which step of risk management?

2.35 Risk Data Sheet: Market Insights Leaders

699. Will revised controls lead to tolerable risk levels?

700. During work activities could hazards exist?

701. Potential for recurrence?

702. What are the main opportunities available to you that you should grab while you can?

703. Has a sensitivity analysis been carried out?

704. What are you here for (Mission)?

705. Who has a vested interest in how you perform as your organization (our stakeholders)?

706. What will be the consequences if it happens?

707. Whom do you serve (customers)?

708. How can it happen?

709. What was measured?

710. Has the most cost-effective solution been chosen?

711. Type of risk identified?

712. What if client refuses?

713. Do effective diagnostic tests exist?

714. What is the environment within which you operate (social trends, economic, community values, broad based participation, national directions etc.)?

715. How reliable is the data source?

716. What will be the consequences if the risk happens?

717. What are you trying to achieve (Objectives)?

2.36 Procurement Management Plan: Market Insights Leaders

718. Are meeting objectives identified for each meeting?

719. Are Market Insights Leaders project team members involved in detailed estimating and scheduling?

720. Does the Market Insights Leaders project team have the right skills?

721. Does all Market Insights Leaders project documentation reside in a common repository for easy access?

722. Have adequate resources been provided by management to ensure Market Insights Leaders project success?

723. What is a Market Insights Leaders project Management Plan?

724. Is there a procurement management plan in place?

725. Are changes in deliverable commitments agreed to by all affected groups & individuals?

726. Are vendor invoices audited for accuracy before payment?

727. Are enough systems & user personnel assigned to the Market Insights Leaders project?

728. Does the Market Insights Leaders project have a Statement of Work?

729. Is there a formal process for updating the Market Insights Leaders project baseline?

730. Are issues raised, assessed, actioned, and resolved in a timely and efficient manner?

731. Is there a requirements change management processes in place?

732. If standardized procurement documents are needed, where can others be found?

733. Has a sponsor been identified?

2.37 Source Selection Criteria: Market Insights Leaders

734. What are the most critical evaluation criteria that prove to be tiebreakers in the evaluation of proposals?

735. How should the solicitation aspects regarding past performance be structured?

736. What does an evaluation address and what does a sample resemble?

737. Which contract type places the most risk on the seller?

738. How do you facilitate evaluation against published criteria?

739. Is there collaboration among your evaluators?

740. Who is on the Source Selection Advisory Committee?

741. What should a DRFP include?

742. What are the steps in performing a cost/tech tradeoff?

743. What documentation is necessary regarding electronic communications?

744. Are evaluators ready to begin this task?

745. Are there any common areas of weaknesses or deficiencies in the proposals in the competitive range?

746. Who is entitled to a debriefing?

747. What management structure does your organization consider as optimal for performing the contract?

748. How are clarifications and communications appropriately used?

749. What should be considered?

750. What risks were identified in the proposals?

751. Have team members been adequately trained?

752. How and when do you enter into Market Insights Leaders project Procurement Management?

753. When is it appropriate to issue a DRFP?

2.38 Stakeholder Management Plan: Market Insights Leaders

754. Do you use diagrams and tables to account for complex concepts and increase overall readability?

755. Will all outputs delivered by the Market Insights Leaders project follow the same process?

756. Have Market Insights Leaders project management standards and procedures been established and documented?

757. Who will perform the review(s)?

758. What inspection and testing is to be performed?

759. Are Market Insights Leaders project leaders committed to this Market Insights Leaders project full time?

760. Are staff skills known and available for each task?

761. Are enough systems & user personnel assigned to the Market Insights Leaders project?

762. What are the procedures and processes to be followed for purchases, including approval and authorisation requirements?

763. Will all relevant stakeholders be included within the review process?

764. Have all involved Market Insights Leaders project stakeholders and work groups committed to the Market Insights Leaders project?

765. Are written status reports provided on a designated frequent basis?

766. How will the equipment be verified?

2.39 Change Management Plan: Market Insights Leaders

767. Do you need a new organization structure?

768. How much change management is needed?

769. How frequently should you repeat the message?

770. What risks may occur upfront?

771. How badly can information be misinterpreted?

772. What will be the preferred method of delivery?

773. Have the approved procedures and policies been published?

774. Are work location changes required?

775. How will you deal with anger about the restricting of communications due to confidentiality considerations?

776. What skills, education, knowledge, or work experiences should the resources have for each identified competency?

777. Do you need a new organizational structure?

778. What is the most positive interpretation it can receive?

779. When does it make sense to customize?

780. Do you need new systems?

781. What new roles are needed?

782. Is there an adequate supply of people for the new roles?

783. Which relationships will change?

784. What is going to be done differently?

785. What work practices will be affected?

786. Do there need to be new channels developed?

3.0 Executing Process Group: Market Insights Leaders

787. How do you prevent staff are just doing busywork to pass the time?

788. How well did the chosen processes produce the expected results?

789. Why should Market Insights Leaders project managers strive to make jobs look easy?

790. What were things that you need to improve?

791. What is the difference between conceptual, application, and evaluative questions?

792. What are the challenges Market Insights Leaders project teams face?

793. When will the Market Insights Leaders project be done?

794. Does the Market Insights Leaders project team have enough people to execute the Market Insights Leaders project plan?

795. What type of people would you want on your team?

796. Could a new application negatively affect the current IT infrastructure?

797. What will you do to minimize the impact should a risk event occur?

798. What are the main types of goods and services being outsourced?

799. How well did the team follow the chosen processes?

800. Who will be the main sponsor?

3.1 Team Member Status Report: Market Insights Leaders

801. How much risk is involved?

802. Are the attitudes of staff regarding Market Insights Leaders project work improving?

803. The problem with Reward & Recognition Programs is that the truly deserving people all too often get left out. How can you make it practical?

804. How will resource planning be done?

805. Does your organization have the means (staff, money, contract, etc.) to produce or to acquire the product, good, or service?

806. What specific interest groups do you have in place?

807. Are your organizations Market Insights Leaders projects more successful over time?

808. Is there evidence that staff is taking a more professional approach toward management of your organizations Market Insights Leaders projects?

809. Are the products of your organizations Market Insights Leaders projects meeting customers objectives?

810. Will the staff do training or is that done by a third

party?

811. Why is it to be done?

812. Does every department have to have a Market Insights Leaders project Manager on staff?

813. Does the product, good, or service already exist within your organization?

814. How can you make it practical?

815. How does this product, good, or service meet the needs of the Market Insights Leaders project and your organization as a whole?

816. When a teams productivity and success depend on collaboration and the efficient flow of information, what generally fails them?

817. How it is to be done?

818. What is to be done?

819. Do you have an Enterprise Market Insights Leaders project Management Office (EPMO)?

3.2 Change Request: Market Insights Leaders

820. Who will perform the change?

821. What can be filed?

822. Should a more thorough impact analysis be conducted?

823. Will all change requests be unconditionally tracked through this process?

824. Has the change been highlighted and documented in the CSCI?

825. Who is included in the change control team?

826. How well do experienced software developers predict software change?

827. Since there are no change requests in your Market Insights Leaders project at this point, what must you have before you begin?

828. Will this change conflict with other requirements changes (e.g., lead to conflicting operational scenarios)?

829. Describe how modifications, enhancements, defects and/or deficiencies shall be notified (e.g. Problem Reports, Change Requests etc) and managed. Detail warranty and/or maintenance

periods?

830. Can you answer what happened, who did it, when did it happen, and what else will be affected?

831. What should be regulated in a change control operating instruction?

832. For which areas does this operating procedure apply?

833. What is the change request log?

834. Change request coordination ?

835. Has your address changed?

836. Why control change across the life cycle?

837. How shall the implementation of changes be recorded?

838. Who has responsibility for approving and ranking changes?

3.3 Change Log: Market Insights Leaders

839. Is the submitted change a new change or a modification of a previously approved change?

840. Will the Market Insights Leaders project fail if the change request is not executed?

841. Is the change request within Market Insights Leaders project scope?

842. Do the described changes impact on the integrity or security of the system?

843. Is this a mandatory replacement?

844. Is the requested change request a result of changes in other Market Insights Leaders project(s)?

845. Is the change backward compatible without limitations?

846. Is the change request open, closed or pending?

847. Who initiated the change request?

848. How does this change affect the timeline of the schedule?

849. How does this relate to the standards developed for specific business processes?

850. How does this change affect scope?

851. When was the request approved?

852. Does the suggested change request seem to represent a necessary enhancement to the product?

853. When was the request submitted?

3.4 Decision Log: Market Insights Leaders

854. Who is the decisionmaker?

855. Adversarial environment. is your opponent open to a non-traditional workflow, or will it likely challenge anything you do?

856. Is everything working as expected?

857. Linked to original objective?

858. What was the rationale for the decision?

859. Behaviors; what are guidelines that the team has identified that will assist them with getting the most out of team meetings?

860. Is your opponent open to a non-traditional workflow, or will it likely challenge anything you do?

861. What alternatives/risks were considered?

862. Who will be given a copy of this document and where will it be kept?

863. Which variables make a critical difference?

864. How do you define success?

865. With whom was the decision shared or considered?

866. What are the cost implications?

867. Does anything need to be adjusted?

868. At what point in time does loss become unacceptable?

869. How do you know when you are achieving it?

870. How effective is maintaining the log at facilitating organizational learning?

871. Decision-making process; how will the team make decisions?

872. How does provision of information, both in terms of content and presentation, influence acceptance of alternative strategies?

873. What is the line where eDiscovery ends and document review begins?

3.5 Quality Audit: Market Insights Leaders

874. Are salvageable and salvaged medical devices stored in a manner to prevent damage and/or contamination?

875. Are there sufficient personnel having the necessary education, background, training, and experience to assure that all operations are correctly performed?

876. Are training programs documented?

877. Does the supplier use a formal quality system?

878. How does your organization know that its promotions system is appropriately effective, constructive and fair?

879. How does your organization know that its staff placements are appropriately effective and constructive in relation to program-related learning outcomes?

880. How does your organization know that the support for its staff is appropriately effective and constructive?

881. What will the Observer get to Observe?

882. How does your organization know that its system for staff performance planning and review is

appropriately effective and constructive?

883. How does your organization know that its system for ensuring that its training activities are appropriately resourced and support is appropriately effective and constructive?

884. How does your organization know that the research supervision provided to its staff is appropriately effective and constructive?

885. Are adequate and conveniently located toilet facilities available for use by the employees?

886. How does your organization know that its system for inducting new staff to maximize workplace contributions are appropriately effective and constructive?

887. How does your organization know that it is maintaining a conducive staff climate?

888. How does your organization know that its relationships with other relevant organizations are appropriately effective and constructive?

889. How does your organization know that its range of activities are being reviewed as rigorously and constructively as they could be?

890. What does an analysis of your organizations staff profile suggest in terms of its planning, and how is this being addressed?

891. Are all staff empowered and encouraged to contribute to ongoing improvement efforts?

892. How does your organization know that the range and quality of its accommodation, catering and transportation services are appropriately effective and constructive?

893. How does your organization know that its risk management system is appropriately effective and constructive?

3.6 Team Directory: Market Insights Leaders

894. What are you going to deliver or accomplish?

895. How do unidentified risks impact the outcome of the Market Insights Leaders project?

896. Who will talk to the customer?

897. Process decisions: which organizational elements and which individuals will be assigned management functions?

898. Timing: when do the effects of communication take place?

899. What needs to be communicated?

900. When does information need to be distributed?

901. Why is the work necessary?

902. Process decisions: do invoice amounts match accepted work in place?

903. Process decisions: how well was task order work performed?

904. Days from the time the issue is identified?

905. Have you decided when to celebrate the Market Insights Leaders projects completion date?

906. Decisions: what could be done better to improve the quality of the constructed product?

907. Where will the product be used and/or delivered or built when appropriate?

908. Who are the Team Members?

909. How will the team handle changes?

910. Who will write the meeting minutes and distribute?

911. Process decisions: do job conditions warrant additional actions to collect job information and document on-site activity?

3.7 Team Operating Agreement: Market Insights Leaders

912. What is culture?

913. Do you leverage technology engagement tools group chat, polls, screen sharing, etc.?

914. Do you record meetings for the already stated unable to attend?

915. Did you prepare participants for the next meeting?

916. Do you use a parking lot for any items that are important and outside of the agenda?

917. Are there differences in access to communication and collaboration technology based on team member location?

918. Resource allocation: how will individual team members account for time and expenses, and how will this be allocated in the team budget?

919. Do you call or email participants to ensure understanding, follow-through and commitment to the meeting outcomes?

920. Do you upload presentation materials in advance and test the technology?

921. Did you draft the meeting agenda?

922. Have you established procedures that team members can follow to work effectively together, such as a team operating agreement?

923. What are some potential sources of conflict among team members?

924. Are there more than two functional areas represented by your team?

925. Did you determine the technology methods that best match the messages to be communicated?

926. What is the anticipated procedure (recruitment, solicitation of volunteers, or assignment) for selecting team members?

927. Methodologies: how will key team processes be implemented, such as training, research, work deliverable production, review and approval processes, knowledge management, and meeting procedures?

928. Communication protocols: how will the team communicate?

929. Do you solicit member feedback about meetings and what would make them better?

930. What resources can be provided for the team in terms of equipment, space, time for training, protected time and space for meetings, and travel allowances?

931. Has the appropriate access to relevant data and

analysis capability been granted?

3.8 Team Performance Assessment: Market Insights Leaders

932. To what degree do all members feel responsible for all agreed-upon measures?

933. To what degree do team members frequently explore the teams purpose and its implications?

934. What are teams?

935. To what degree is the team cognizant of small wins to be celebrated along the way?

936. To what degree do team members articulate the teams work approach?

937. To what degree do team members understand one anothers roles and skills?

938. To what degree do the goals specify concrete team work products?

939. To what degree are the teams goals and objectives clear, simple, and measurable?

940. To what degree does the team possess adequate membership to achieve its ends?

941. What is method variance?

942. What do you think is the most constructive thing that could be done now to resolve considerations and

disputes about method variance?

943. Social categorization and intergroup behaviour: Does minimal intergroup discrimination make social identity more positive?

944. To what degree will new and supplemental skills be introduced as the need is recognized?

945. To what degree do team members feel that the purpose of the team is important, if not exciting?

946. To what degree are corresponding categories of skills either actually or potentially represented across the membership?

947. To what degree does the teams work approach provide opportunity for members to engage in results-based evaluation?

948. To what degree are the relative importance and priority of the goals clear to all team members?

949. To what degree can team members meet frequently enough to accomplish the teams ends?

950. Do friends perform better than acquaintances?

951. Where to from here?

3.9 Team Member Performance Assessment: Market Insights Leaders

952. Who receives a benchmark visit?

953. Is there reluctance to join a team?

954. What are they responsible for?

955. How are training activities developed from a technical perspective?

956. To what degree can the team measure progress against specific goals?

957. To what extent are systems and applications (e.g., game engine, mobile device platform) utilized?

958. How is assessment information achieved, stored?

959. To what degree are sub-teams possible or necessary?

960. How accurately is your plan implemented?

961. Who should attend?

962. What are the key duties or tasks of the Ratee?

963. What is the target group for instruction (e.g., individual and collective or small team instruction)?

964. What evaluation results did you have?

965. How do you use data to inform instruction and improve staff achievement?

966. What kinds of performance factors / elements do you use?

967. How do you determine which data are the most important to use, analyze, or review?

968. Are assessment validation activities performed?

3.10 Issue Log: Market Insights Leaders

969. Why multiple evaluators?

970. Which team member will work with each stakeholder?

971. Who is the issue assigned to?

972. In classifying stakeholders, which approach to do so are you using?

973. How do you reply to this question; you am new here and managing this major program. How do you suggest you build your network?

974. What are the typical contents?

975. What approaches do you use?

976. What are the stakeholders interrelationships?

977. Are the stakeholders getting the information they need, are they consulted, are concerns addressed?

978. Is access to the Issue Log controlled?

979. Persistence; will users learn a work around or will they be bothered every time?

980. Who reported the issue?

981. What is a change?

982. Do you often overlook a key stakeholder or stakeholder group?

983. Why do you manage human resources?

4.0 Monitoring and Controlling Process Group: Market Insights Leaders

984. Where is the Risk in the Market Insights Leaders project?

985. How many more potential communications channels were introduced by the discovery of the new stakeholders?

986. What areas were overlooked on this Market Insights Leaders project?

987. Mitigate. what will you do to minimize the impact should a risk event occur?

988. Do the products created live up to the necessary quality?

989. What is the timeline for the Market Insights Leaders project?

990. Is there adequate validation on required fields?

991. How is agile portfolio management done?

992. How are you doing?

993. Is there sufficient funding available for this?

994. When will the Market Insights Leaders project be done?

995. How is agile program management done?

996. Is there undesirable impact on staff or resources?

997. What do they need to know about the Market Insights Leaders project?

998. What kinds of things in particular are you looking for data on?

999. Where is the Risk in the Market Insights Leaders project?

1000. How can you monitor progress?

1001. Who needs to be engaged upfront to ensure use of results?

4.1 Project Performance Report: Market Insights Leaders

1002. Next Steps?

1003. To what degree do individual skills and abilities match task demands?

1004. To what degree is there a sense that only the team can succeed?

1005. To what degree can the team ensure that all members are individually and jointly accountable for the teams purpose, goals, approach, and work-products?

1006. To what degree do team members agree with the goals, relative importance, and the ways in which achievement will be measured?

1007. To what degree does the teams work approach provide opportunity for members to engage in open interaction?

1008. To what degree does the formal organization make use of individual resources and meet individual needs?

1009. To what degree does the funding match the requirement?

1010. To what degree do the structures of the formal organization motivate taskrelevant behavior and facilitate task completion?

1011. To what degree can all members engage in open and interactive considerations?

1012. To what degree does the task meet individual needs?

1013. To what degree are the demands of the task compatible with and converge with the relationships of the informal organization?

1014. What is the PRS?

1015. To what degree are the goals realistic?

1016. To what degree are the structures of the formal organization consistent with the behaviors in the informal organization?

1017. How is the data used?

1018. To what degree can team members vigorously define the teams purpose in considerations with others who are not part of the functioning team?

4.2 Variance Analysis: Market Insights Leaders

1019. Why do variances exist?

1020. Are all budgets assigned to control accounts?

1021. Are the requirements for all items of overhead established by rational, traceable processes?

1022. Are procedures for variance analysis documented and consistently applied at the control account level and selected WBS and organizational levels at least monthly as a routine task?

1023. Contract line items and end items?

1024. Does the contractor use objective results, design reviews and tests to trace schedule performance?

1025. Are data elements reconcilable between internal summary reports and reports forwarded to the stakeholders?

1026. How does the monthly budget compare to the actual experience?

1027. How do you evaluate the impact of schedule changes, work around, et?

1028. How do you identify potential or actual overruns and underruns?

1029. How do you identify and isolate causes of favorable and unfavorable cost and schedule variances?

1030. What business event causes fluctuations?

1031. Are there changes in the overhead pool and/or organization structures?

1032. Are the actual costs used for variance analysis reconcilable with data from the accounting system?

1033. Why are standard cost systems used?

1034. Are work packages assigned to performing organizations?

1035. Who are responsible for overhead performance control of related costs?

1036. There are detailed schedules which support control account and work package start and completion dates/events?

1037. What can be the cause of an increase in costs?

4.3 Earned Value Status: Market Insights Leaders

1038. Earned value can be used in almost any Market Insights Leaders project situation and in almost any Market Insights Leaders project environment. it may be used on large Market Insights Leaders projects, medium sized Market Insights Leaders projects, tiny Market Insights Leaders projects (in cut-down form), complex and simple Market Insights Leaders projects and in any market sector. some people, of course, know all about earned value, they have used it for years - but perhaps not as effectively as they could have?

1039. When is it going to finish?

1040. Verification is a process of ensuring that the developed system satisfies the stakeholders agreements and specifications; Are you building the product right? What do you verify?

1041. What is the unit of forecast value?

1042. Validation is a process of ensuring that the developed system will actually achieve the stakeholders desired outcomes; Are you building the right product? What do you validate?

1043. Where are your problem areas?

1044. How much is it going to cost by the finish?

1045. How does this compare with other Market Insights Leaders projects?

1046. Where is evidence-based earned value in your organization reported?

1047. If earned value management (EVM) is so good in determining the true status of a Market Insights Leaders project and Market Insights Leaders project its completion, why is it that hardly any one uses it in information systems related Market Insights Leaders projects?

1048. Are you hitting your Market Insights Leaders projects targets?

4.4 Risk Audit: Market Insights Leaders

1049. Do you record and file all audits?

1050. Do you have a clear plan for the future that describes what you want to do and how you are going to do it?

1051. Is all required equipment available?

1052. If applicable; are compilers and code generators available and suitable for the product to be built?

1053. Can analytical tests provide evidence that is as strong as evidence from traditional substantive tests?

1054. Is the customer willing to establish rapid communication links with the developer?

1055. Do end-users have realistic expectations?

1056. Does your organization have any policies or procedures to guide its decision-making (code of conduct for the board, conflict of interest policy, etc.)?

1057. Do the people have the right combinations of skills?

1058. What expertise does the Board have on quality, outcomes, and errors?

1059. To what extent are auditors influenced by

the business risk assessment in the audit process, and how can auditors create more effective mental models to more fully examine contradictory evidence?

1060. Does the team have the right mix of skills?

1061. What is the anticipated volatility of the requirements?

1062. Will participants be required to sign a legally counselled waiver or risk disclaimer when entering an event?

1063. What are the Internal Controls ?

1064. How can the strategy fail/achieved?

1065. Will safety checks of personal equipment supplied by competitors be conducted?

1066. Does the Market Insights Leaders project team have experience with the technology to be implemented?

4.5 Contractor Status Report: Market Insights Leaders

1067. What was the actual budget or estimated cost for your organizations services?

1068. What process manages the contracts?

1069. If applicable; describe your standard schedule for new software version releases. Are new software version releases included in the standard maintenance plan?

1070. What was the budget or estimated cost for your organizations services?

1071. What was the overall budget or estimated cost?

1072. How is risk transferred?

1073. Are there contractual transfer concerns?

1074. How long have you been using the services?

1075. What was the final actual cost?

1076. Who can list a Market Insights Leaders project as organization experience, your organization or a previous employee of your organization?

1077. What is the average response time for answering a support call?

1078. What are the minimum and optimal bandwidth requirements for the proposed solution?

1079. Describe how often regular updates are made to the proposed solution. Are corresponding regular updates included in the standard maintenance plan?

4.6 Formal Acceptance: Market Insights Leaders

1080. What function(s) does it fill or meet?

1081. Was business value realized?

1082. Did the Market Insights Leaders project achieve its MOV?

1083. Was the sponsor/customer satisfied?

1084. Does it do what Market Insights Leaders project team said it would?

1085. Was the Market Insights Leaders project goal achieved?

1086. Is formal acceptance of the Market Insights Leaders project product documented and distributed?

1087. What features, practices, and processes proved to be strengths or weaknesses?

1088. Do you buy pre-configured systems or build your own configuration?

1089. General estimate of the costs and times to complete the Market Insights Leaders project?

1090. What lessons were learned about your Market Insights Leaders project management methodology?

1091. Have all comments been addressed?

1092. How does your team plan to obtain formal acceptance on your Market Insights Leaders project?

1093. What are the requirements against which to test, Who will execute?

1094. Was the Market Insights Leaders project managed well?

1095. Does it do what client said it would?

1096. What was done right?

1097. Do you buy-in installation services?

1098. Who would use it?

1099. What can you do better next time?

5.0 Closing Process Group: Market Insights Leaders

1100. How dependent is the Market Insights Leaders project on other Market Insights Leaders projects or work efforts?

1101. Is this an updated Market Insights Leaders project Proposal Document?

1102. Did the Market Insights Leaders project management methodology work?

1103. Contingency planning. if a risk event occurs, what will you do?

1104. What were the actual outcomes?

1105. What were the desired outcomes?

1106. Did the Market Insights Leaders project team have the right skills?

1107. What areas were overlooked on this Market Insights Leaders project?

1108. What were things that you did very well and want to do the same again on the next Market Insights Leaders project?

1109. Were cost budgets met?

1110. How well did the chosen processes fit the needs

of the Market Insights Leaders project?

1111. Were sponsors and decision makers available when needed outside regularly scheduled meetings?

1112. How will staff learn how to use the deliverables?

1113. What areas were overlooked on this Market Insights Leaders project?

5.1 Procurement Audit: Market Insights Leaders

1114. Has guidelines been set up for how the procurement function/unit should carry out its procurements?

1115. Are the rules for automatic payment in computer programs approved by management prior to implementation?

1116. Is trend analysis performed on expenditures made by key employees and by vendor?

1117. Did the contracting authority verify compliance with the basic requirements of the competition?

1118. When corresponding references were made, was a precise description of the performance not otherwise possible and were the already stated references accompanied by the words or equivalent?

1119. Is there a system in place to handle partial delivery of orders, back orders, and partial payments?

1120. Did your organization calculate the contract value accurately?

1121. Was the award criterion only the most economical advantageous tender?

1122. Were the specifications of the contract determined free from influence of particular interests of consultants, experts or other economic operators?

1123. Are contract changes after awarding properly justified and executed?

1124. Is free and fair (international) competition promoted by organizational policies and legislation, in line with legal, trade organizations and other policies?

1125. Is the minutes book kept current?

1126. Were exclusion causes duly considered before the actual evaluation of tenders?

1127. Where applicable, did your organization adequately manage experts employed to assist in the procurement process?

1128. Are all purchase orders accounted for?

1129. Audits: when was your last independent public accountant (ipa) audit and what were the results?

1130. Has your organization procedures in place to monitor the input of experts employed to assist the procurement function?

1131. Is the relationship between in-house and external work considered in the strategy?

1132. Is there no evidence of collusion between bidders?

1133. Has your organization clearly defined the award criteria?

5.2 Contract Close-Out: Market Insights Leaders

1134. Have all acceptance criteria been met prior to final payment to contractors?

1135. How does it work?

1136. Parties: Authorized?

1137. What is capture management?

1138. Has each contract been audited to verify acceptance and delivery?

1139. Change in attitude or behavior?

1140. How is the contracting office notified of the automatic contract close-out?

1141. What happens to the recipient of services?

1142. Are the signers the authorized officials?

1143. Was the contract sufficiently clear so as not to result in numerous disputes and misunderstandings?

1144. Have all contract records been included in the Market Insights Leaders project archives?

1145. Was the contract complete without requiring numerous changes and revisions?

1146. Was the contract type appropriate?

1147. Change in circumstances?

1148. Change in knowledge?

1149. Why Outsource?

1150. How/when used ?

1151. Have all contracts been closed?

1152. Parties: who is involved?

1153. Have all contracts been completed?

5.3 Project or Phase Close-Out: Market Insights Leaders

1154. How often did each stakeholder need an update?

1155. What information is each stakeholder group interested in?

1156. Is there a clear cause and effect between the activity and the lesson learned?

1157. What were the goals and objectives of the communications strategy for the Market Insights Leaders project?

1158. Planned completion date?

1159. What are the mandatory communication needs for each stakeholder?

1160. What can you do better next time, and what specific actions can you take to improve?

1161. Who are the Market Insights Leaders project stakeholders and what are roles and involvement?

1162. What is this stakeholder expecting?

1163. How much influence did the stakeholder have over others?

1164. What was the preferred delivery mechanism?

1165. What process was planned for managing issues/risks?

1166. What is in it for you?

1167. What information did each stakeholder need to contribute to the Market Insights Leaders projects success?

1168. What are the informational communication needs for each stakeholder?

1169. Which changes might a stakeholder be required to make as a result of the Market Insights Leaders project?

1170. What hierarchical authority does the stakeholder have in your organization?

1171. Is the lesson based on actual Market Insights Leaders project experience rather than on independent research?

1172. Who controlled the resources for the Market Insights Leaders project?

5.4 Lessons Learned: Market Insights Leaders

1173. How much communication is socially oriented?

1174. Was the control overhead justified?

1175. What regulatory constraints impact the case?

1176. How much communication is task-related?

1177. Can the lesson learned be replicated?

1178. Was the schedule met?

1179. How to write up the lesson identified – how will you document the results of your analysis corresponding that you have an li ready to take the next step in the ll process?

1180. How complete and timely were the materials you were provided to decide whether to proceed from one Market Insights Leaders project lifecycle phase to the next?

1181. Do you have any real problems?

1182. What were the key issues?

1183. How well did the Market Insights Leaders project Manager respond to questions or comments related to the Market Insights Leaders project?

1184. How objective was the collection of data?

1185. Overall, how effective was the performance of the Market Insights Leaders project Manager?

1186. How satisfied are you with your involvement in the development and/or review of the Market Insights Leaders project Scope during Market Insights Leaders project Initiation and Planning?

1187. What mistakes did you successfully avoid making?

1188. What is the frequency of personal communications?

1189. How well do you feel the executives supported this Market Insights Leaders project?

1190. How was the political and social history changed over the life of the Market Insights Leaders project?

1191. How was the quality of products/processes assured?

1192. How effective were Market Insights Leaders project audits?

Index

272

CPSIA information can be obtained
at www.ICGtesting.com
Printed in the USA
BVHW041011200819
556236BV00011B/725/P